THE LEAST LIKELY MILLIONAIRE

The Least Likely

MILLIONAIRE

How to **Succeed** When Everyone
Expects You to Fail

JONATHAN BESKIN

MERIDIAN
PUBLISHING

THE LEAST LIKELY MILLIONAIRE
How to Succeed When Everyone Expects You to Fail
First Edition

ISBN 978-1-5445-4346-8 *Hardcover*
    978-1-5445-4344-4 *Paperback*
    978-1-5445-4345-1 *Ebook*
    978-1-5445-4347-5 *Audiobook*

To all the haters and doubters: thank you.

AUTHOR'S NOTE

Many of the names in this story have been
changed as a courtesy.

CONTENTS

INTRODUCTION

For one brief moment in high school, I was the center of the universe.

I was a senior, surrounded by hundreds of kids who had come to see me. It felt like all of Spanish River High School was there, packed into a local park near The Colonnade. This was a beautiful community, so everything was perfect: blue sky, crisp palms, and manicured lawns. The kids who formed the circle around me were beautiful, too, with girls in designer skirts and expensive haircuts standing next to boys who drove fast cars and never worried about how much it cost to fill their gas tanks.

But I couldn't see any of that. All I saw was Evan Engold standing in front of me, fists up, ready to swing.

I had talked a big game to get here. A couple days before, at a school assembly, I opened my mouth and made some wisecrack about one of the guys on the gym floor. I probably called him an asshole—or worse. I hated school and had no patience for assemblies, so it didn't matter who the guy was or what he was doing I would have hated it and hated him for being out there, talented, and happy.

I was neither of those things, so I shot my mouth off.

But it did matter to Evan, who was sitting in the row of bleachers in front of me. He turned around and looked me dead in the eye. "That's my friend, and you gotta watch what you say."

Now I had to be a tough guy. "Go fuck yourself," I responded.

So there I was, the star of a show I had no business being in. I had never been in a fight, and I didn't know what I was doing. My mom was a kindergarten teacher, and my dad hadn't been around since I was six, so it's not like anyone ever taught me to defend myself. But I was there now, and I had to win. I couldn't let all these screaming kids get what they came for: to see me go down.

Evan threw the first punch. He hit me square in the jaw.

I staggered backwards, disoriented. I looked around the faces of the kids watching were blurry for a minute. My face was burning, and though I could see the crowd around me yelling,

I couldn't hear them. All I heard was my own blood pounding in my ears.

My heart was beating fast, and I broke into a sweat. I felt the muscles in my shoulders and neck tightening. I clenched my fists.

But before I could do anything, Evan hit me again. And again. And again.

I was his punching bag.

And there was nothing I could do about it.

When I think about that fight today, I still feel the tension creep into my body. I get a little lightheaded, and it's like I'm seventeen again, wanting so badly to prove myself to the rich kids of Boca Raton. All the pain comes rushing back—not just the physical cuts and bruises but the emotional ones. That fight left no doubt in anyone's mind that I was the laughing stock of Spanish River High School, a loser who drove a shitty car, wore cheap clothes, and lived in a duplex well outside of the gated communities and golf clubs everyone else enjoyed.

I was never good enough, and to the families of Boca, I never would be.

NEVER ENOUGH

Even in my earliest memories, I always knew I was different. When I was five, my father was indicted on charges of insurance fraud. An engineer by trade, he opened a few liquor stores when he and my mother moved to Boca Raton. When one of them burned down, my father was tried and convicted of the crime. I have very few memories of that time, and it wasn't until I was an adult that I understood the full story. But as a young child, I remember my parents sitting me down to tell me that Dad was going away, and I wouldn't see him for a little bit.

The little bit stretched into much longer, though, as my parents divorced soon after his conviction. My father was in a minimum security prison for about six months, but after that, he never paid my mom child support. After he was released from prison, my dad never returned to our family, so I had no one to guide me. I never experienced having a dad who took me to work with him or showed me how to do things around the house. He never even taught me how to throw a baseball.

My mom was left on her own to raise me; she worked as a kindergarten teacher at the local schools, taking on extra work in the after-school daycare program to make sure we kept a roof over our heads and food on our plates.

For most of my life growing up, it was just the two of us. My mom was my only family, and because she was working from seven in the morning until six o'clock every night, I was left on my own a lot. In elementary school, it didn't really bother me that my mom drove a used car and that when we went to the mall, I couldn't have the nicest clothes or toys, but, as I grew older, those differences were always there.

And other people definitely noticed. For starters, my mom was single, and since she dared to date, people talked. When I was seven or eight, I played on a youth baseball team in town. This was a step up from tee ball, where one of the coaches would lob the ball in for the kids to hit. It's actually not easy to slow-pitch to little kids, and the guy who took on that job for my team was dating my mom. When they broke up halfway through the season, he stopped coming to the games. I don't remember much about the guy, but I do remember that all the other parents were upset to lose such a good pitcher—and I remember hearing them talk about us in the bleachers. Their whispers and their frowns made it clear that there was something wrong with me and my mom.

We didn't belong.

As I got older, I became more attuned to the fact that the families in the gated communities of Boca Raton looked down on us. By middle school, if I was hanging out with a group of kids and someone got in trouble, I always got blamed. Kids called me "trailer trash," and their parents expected the worst of me.

Even with kids I considered friends, there was always an invisible line between us. During a synagogue youth group trip to Israel, I grew close to a boy named Josh Lewis, who was also in my grade at school. We hung out frequently (always at his house, never at mine), and though I could never join him on holiday ski trips or Saturdays on his family boat, we spent a lot of time together.

But every time his mother, Sharon, stepped into the room, I felt the judgment radiating off of her. She would plaster on a fake smile, cock her head and ask, "Jonathan, how's your mother? I heard she was *dating*...?"

From passive-aggressive parents to kids slinging rumors that I lived in a trailer park, I struggled for years with the feeling that I was *less than*: less wealthy, less intelligent, less cool, less worthy. That feeling made me act out in all kinds of ways, from smoking lots of pot to trying to deck out my lime green Mazda Protege with strobe lights and a massive exhaust pipe. By the time I got to high school, I was sure that everyone was talking about me behind my back, making fun of me for where I lived and all the things I didn't have. So I poured plenty of gasoline on those fires by shooting my mouth off.

That chip on my shoulder is what got me into that fight that day in the park, and it weighed me down through the rest of high school and my adult life. It even followedme right into the psychiatric hospital where I was ultimately treated for debilitating anxiety and depression.

But that chip on my shoulder is also what got me where I am today. Because through it all, my burning desire to prove the haters wrong is what fueled me to make more of my life—to do something so big that all those rich kids would have to sit up and take notice.

And that's exactly what I did. Starting my own company from nothing but an idea and a few social media hashtags and built it into a world-renowned brand, generating over **$60 million in revenue and over $15 million in profit** in just six years. SinglesSwag has been ranked twice on the *Inc.* **5000 list of the Fastest-Growing Private Companies in America.** In 2020, we cracked the Top 200 on the *Inc.* list, putting us in rare company. (To put that in perspective, Microsoft, Under Armour, Zappos, and Patagonia were also ranked in the Top 200 in their early days.)

SinglesSwag has proudly **shipped more than 2.5 million boxes to 350,000 customers in more than fifty countries.** We've also cultivated a community of over **2 million verified social media followers**—and I did it all without ever raising a penny from outside investors. I didn't have help from a fancy executive team, outside agencies, or boutique PR firms. It was just me, my idea, and my determination to succeed.

This is the story of how I did it, and what I learned along the way.

WHAT'S IN IT FOR YOU?

For a long time, my problem was that I believed all the things people told me about myself. I believed the baseball parents when they hinted that I had ruined the season for the team. I believed the other kids' parents when they said I was a bad kid who led their children straight into trouble. I believed all the teachers who said I wasn't smart enough and would never amount to anything.

I also believed all the conventional wisdom and advice that people doled out about my career:

- "Stick to that company no matter what—it takes time to move up the corporate ladder."
- "You're only worth what they'll pay you."
- "You have to wait to prove yourself for that promotion."
- "You can't start your own business—you don't know what you're doing."
- "That crazy idea will never work—it's a total joke."

- "You don't have the skills to run your own company."
- "You'll never be able to launch a serious business without investors, and no one is going to give *you* any money."

For far too long, I felt stuck in my life and powerless to change.

Perhaps you've felt that way, too. You want to change your life and do something that really means something. You might want to start your own side hustle or build a business to break out of the rut of having someone else control your success. You want to be successful and happy, but something is holding you back.

Your problems could be the same as mine:

- **No connections**: You don't come from a wealthy or famous family, and you didn't attend a prestigious university with a big alumni network full of people ready to help you.

- **No money**: You don't have extra savings to invest in your idea—in fact, you may be barely getting by in your day job.

- **No credentials**: You don't have a fancy degree or distinguished corporate background with expertise in marketing, finance, manufacturing, or any other relevant areas.

- **No self-esteem:** You see successful entrepreneurs on TV or read about them in books and just *know* that they have something you don't. You're not glamorous, rich, or smart enough to ever do what they do.

- **No time:** You face real challenges in your life—family issues, struggles with mental health including anxiety and depression, financial challenges that keep you trapped in your day job—and can't imagine how you could possibly have the time or energy to start a business on top of all that.

- **No support:** You've been told, either to your face or behind your back, that you are not good enough to be successful. And there's a part of you that believes it.

I'm here to tell you that I've been where you are right now. I was the ultimate underdog, taking punches and getting mad about it—but unable to make the leap.

But then, one day, I did.

And it worked.

In this book, I hope to inspire you with my story. It's definitely not the typical success story that you read about in the *Wall*

Street Journal, where a dude with an idea sells it to a bunch of investors and makes millions overnight. This is also not a step-by-step guide about how to build a company. This is an honest look at some of the darkest places in my life, and how I climbed out of that hole to build something great. It's the story of how I overcame a lifetime of anxiety and depression by channeling it into a healthy obsession—and how I turned that obsession into a life-changing success.

Along the way, I'll share what I learned—about myself and about navigating the business world as an outsider. I'll also point out all the terrible advice that I got to show you that so **much of the conventional wisdom around entrepreneurship is total bullshit.** You don't have to keep listening to the voices that keep telling you "No." **You have the power to forge your own path.**

None of my success happened overnight, and none of it came easily. But it *did* happen—and it can happen for you, too. You can get courageous in the face of adversity and commit to your dream.

You *can* do it.

CHAPTER 1

ASLEEP AT THE WHEEL

As usual, the fluorescent lights bathed my office in a bluish-white glow. As usual, the collar of my shirt was digging into my neck. As usual, the distant sound of the money-counting machine fluttered beneath the dull purr of the air conditioner. Everything was in its place—in its excruciatingly predictable place.

The only thing out of place was the guy pointing a gun at one of my tellers.

It was the winter of 2006, and I was managing a branch of SunTrust Bank in Washington, DC. While I helped a customer in the lobby, a man in a puffy jacket, black ski hat, and sunglasses strolled across the floor and passed the teller a note demanding all the money in her drawer.

He never said a word.

As soon as the robber walked out, the nineteen-year-old teller left her window and approached me. Her stride was swift, but her hands were shaking. "Lock the doors," she said.

This was the code word for a robbery, and I was the one in charge. I was rattled, but I couldn't take a time-out to de-stress. As the manager, I had to follow a strict protocol, and the investigation procedures kicked in immediately. The teller who was the target of the robbery had to be isolated from the other employees, the FBI had to be called in, and every employee had to be interviewed separately. In these cases, the FBI routinely checks for any signs of an inside job.

Even though the robber never pointed his gun directly at me, that day was a hellish experience. Everyone at the branch was deeply shaken.

The agents peppered us with questions, and then gave each other skeptical little side glances as we stumbled through our sincere responses. I had just been through one of the scariest things that had ever happened to me, and on top of it all I was made to feel like a criminal. My stomach churned, and a cold trickle of sweat ran down my back.

We were interviewed and eventually dismissed eleven hours later, left to wander out of the dark cave of the bank and into the cold night. When I got to my car, I just sat. I had no idea where to go or what to do next.

I have to get out of this job, I thought.

Even when we weren't being robbed, I was discontent. "Branch manager" might sound like a position of authority, but in a company of over 1,200 branches, managers like me were a dime a dozen. My title certainly didn't command respect in the company. In fact, in terms of the corporate ladder, I was near the bottom.

At twenty-five years old, I was also one of the youngest branch managers at SunTrust, and struggled to gain the respect of the forty- and even fifty-somethings I managed. Without feeling valued by the executives above me or the employees under me, I was already looking for an exit. The robbery just pushed me towards the door.

Explaining direct deposits or wire transfers wasn't my true calling, and I definitely didn't enjoy the subtle but endless social demands of managing people. Quitting after being robbed at gunpoint should have been a no-brainer, right? But even after that awful day, I didn't set out on my own. I didn't even *consider* starting my own business. Banking was what I did, and it's what people expected me to do. With average grades from an average college, it's all I knew how to do. There was no way I could land anything better.

So when I hit the want ads, I looked for another job in—you guessed it—*banking*.

Looking back on that time, I can see that I was blind to all the possibilities that existed outside of my limited world. I can see that I was ignoring thousands of other paths that I might have found more fulfilling. But I just didn't know better. I had no one to guide me. I never had a role model to teach me about career opportunities or help me discover my strengths. And passions? Those were for people who already had money and connections.

I needed a mentor. But when you grow up like I did, it's not like people are lining up to lend you a helping hand.

ADRIFT

My mother worked very hard to raise me the best that she could on her own, but she worked almost twelve hours a day, so I was on my own for several hours after school, almost every day. I had no siblings to play with, and I had very few friends. And as I grew older, I realized that I didn't fit in with the other kids of

Boca Raton. While they were off taking private French lessons and learning to play polo, I was eating Doritos and watching reruns of *The Brady Bunch* after school.

By the time I hit my teen years, reruns from the '70s weren't cutting it anymore. I needed more interaction, and I started acting out to get attention. I got my tongue pierced and got a tattoo. I flew the flag of rebellion to stand out in the uptight, carefully manicured world of Boca Raton. When I did attract a few running mates, I still felt the need to show off. I stole my mom's car for a trip to the beach with friends before I was old enough to drive.

I felt like I had to pull some pretty crazy stunts to get people to like me. Maybe I was trying to fill the void left by my absent father. Maybe I just wanted some friends. Whatever the reason, it was pushing my mom to her limit. So when I was sixteen, she shipped me off to live with an aunt in New Jersey. After a few months, my aunt shipped me right back.

I was rudderless.

When my mom fell in love again and remarried, I didn't click with the guy. Big shock—a teenager who doesn't get along with his stepdad. Instead of becoming a much-needed source of guidance for me, the new relationship became contentious. We fought often, sometimes physically, and I once pushed him so far that he called the police on me.

The only coaching I received during those years was from my stepdad's twenty-year-old son, who gave me detailed lessons on how to smoke pot.

I was only fourteen.

Within a year or two, my stepdad split up with my mom and left us, taking a chunk of our money with him. I'm sure Sharon Lewis had a field day gossiping about us at the Woodcrest Country Club.

It wasn't just the lack of a father figure driving my rebellious behavior. I also suffered from severe anxiety and depression. My mom sent me to a psychiatrist, hoping that medication might help get me back on the right track, but we never found the right combination of meds and dosages. At one particularly low point, while we were adjusting my medications, it was determined that I was a potential danger to myself and I ended up being hospitalized for a week in an out-patient program.

Every morning, a white van would pick me up and drive to a secure facility where there were group discussions, activities, and individual therapy. It wasn't bad at first, but there were very strict protocols about where you could go and what you could do without permission.

One day during a group therapy session, something happened that upset me. I can't remember what it was, but I do remember that I stood up and started walking toward the door. I just wanted to step out for some air and to get away from the other kids. What could be more normal than walking away from a person you didn't want to be with?

Suddenly, adults were everywhere, running and shouting, "Code White! Code White!" I would later learn that this was a code to identify a potentially (or actively) violent or out-of-control individual. A siren pierced the air.

Before I could turn around, a burly man had his arms around me and pinned me against the wall. I was terrified. I tried to get away, but hospital staff wrestled me to the ground and placed me in restraints. They placed me in a bright white room with padded walls, alone.

I was given an injection, and I fell asleep.

I don't remember exactly what happened when they finally let me out of the room, but I'll never forget what the psychiatrist said to my mom when she picked me up: "Jonathan will never be able to return to a school setting or live a normal life. You need to prepare for him to be in an institution, or else he will end up in jail or dead. There is no hope for him to succeed in a traditional setting."

That stung. Actually, it was worse than a sting. It was like the psychiatrist opened my teenage chest and shoved an all-consuming black hole into it. There was no hope for me? All the social exclusion, all of the beatings and bullying from my peers, all of the emptiness and sadness that I felt over my dad not being around…there was no light at the end of that tunnel? I was doomed to a life of endless group therapy and orderlies and padded cells if I got a little too upset for them to handle?

When I returned for therapy the next day, all of the nurses and orderlies looked at me differently. They never smiled, and I could see in their eyes that they didn't want to deal with me. They thought I was a lost cause. They were supposed to be helping me, but they had all given up on me—just like every other teacher and coach in Boca who was supposed to be looking out for me but ended up looking down on me.

I was supposed to leave the out-patient program with more confidence and a better mindset, but I had never felt so worthless.

Despite all of these troubles, I managed to graduate high school on time. I set off for college but had no idea what I should study. I was treading water for the first few semesters until the dean's office informed me that I couldn't remain an "undeclared" major for my entire college career. And so, without any coaching, I chose something that sounded like maybe, just maybe, it could get me what I wanted: enough money to tell all the kids at Spanish River High School to go to hell.

I decided to major in finance.

TAKING THE WHEEL

With no clear guidance from anyone in my life, I grabbed the steering wheel myself. Of course, I had no idea where I was headed.

I had no clue what a finance career was really about. It just sounded glamorous and powerful, and that's what I wanted—I would do anything to show people that I was *worth* something. It wasn't until I graduated college and joined Bank of America's management training program that I started to have an inkling of what I had signed up for. My next job, a business banking position with HSBC, ended badly. I was let go after only seven months *without warning*. I probably deserved to be fired—I was a cocky young guy at the time—but the abrupt, rude firing was a slap in the face, a wake-up call to what the banking industry was really like.

But I didn't wake up. I didn't realize that banking wasn't a great fit for me. Instead, I relocated to DC for that branch manager job at SunTrust. I was never crazy about the job, especially after the robbery, but without any mentoring, I couldn't think outside of the box. I just couldn't see past the path that I was already on.

Plus, after the chaos of my youth, I finally had some stability, and I was afraid to leave it.

All of the evidence from my childhood pointed in the same direction—that taking risks never paid off. The one time in my life I stood up to fight, I got beat down. The one time I tried a change of scenery, my aunt sent me back home. Even other people's risks—like my mother's second marriage—always seemed to end badly. Taking chances was rarely rewarded.

So as an adult, I didn't have the courage to take the leap into something new or different.

I always felt that I was capable of doing more. I knew that I was smart enough for bigger and better things, even if my teachers would have rolled their eyes at the thought. But I lacked the courage to do anything about it. I should have considered entrepreneurship, where I could go as far as my intellect and abilities could carry me. But I always made excuses. I listened to conventional norms. Starting my own business was beyond my wildest dreams.

And that's where it stayed for a long while.

And so, even though I was steering my own life at that point, I wasn't listening to my own needs and wants. Not only did I *not* venture into entrepreneurship, I didn't even try to get a gig outside of the banking world.

Hell, I didn't even venture outside of SunTrust. After the robbery, I kept my job search to the internal postings and hoped for something better.

I got married, had a kid, and went to work every day.

I was in the driver's seat, but I was asleep at the wheel.

DAYDREAMING AT NIGHT

My safe, inside-the-box job search led me to a new job that was one rung up the ladder at SunTrust.

I served as a sales rep in a program called "SunTrust at Work." I coordinated with the employers of the area—anything from small shops to giant government contractors like Raytheon—to sell SunTrust's products and services directly to their employees at their places of business. I set up events at their facilities and talked to people about the different accounts, lines of credit, and benefits that SunTrust could offer them.

This wasn't fulfilling work, but at least it was a new challenge, and it was interesting for a while. I wasn't skyrocketing toward a CEO position, but I did pick up a few skills, such as public speaking, which would serve me well later in my career. The overall problem was that I was still in a lower-level position, and I knew that I was capable of much more. I knew the job wasn't tapping into my true potential, and would never change my life financially; I knew that I was capable of much more, but wasn't sure how to get there.

In a few years, I transferred from the DC area to an identical SunTrust position back in Boca Raton. Suddenly, I was right back where I started, surrounded by the same people who had always made it a point to put me in my place. Every day I drove past neighborhoods I could only hope to live in, and at temple I had to smile and nod while the big shots talked about their European vacations and million-dollar business deals.

The move brought back all of the old feelings. Feeling out of place. Feeling that everyone was more successful than I was.

Feeling that I could never get the life I wanted and deserved. Every night, lying in bed, I fantasized about a bigger, better lifestyle. I dreamed of driving a convertible, moving into the newest gated community, and showing these Boca assholes that I was every bit as good as they were.

To make matters worse, there was little difference between the entitled brats who I grew up with and the condescending executives of the banking world. Many of those banking hotshots looked down on everyone below them in the corporate hierarchy. They treated us as less capable or less intelligent than they were. I daydreamed about these smug execs seeing me on the news someday. I wanted them to see me running a company and making far more money than they had ever made. I wanted to prove something to anyone who had ever doubted me.

It was clear that the scars of my youth hadn't entirely healed.

It didn't help my confidence that my marriage was breaking up. And it certainly didn't help that I was in my thirties and living back with my mother in her house. I stayed up late, obsessively browsing listings for houses I couldn't afford, dreaming of millions but working at a job that barely paid the bills. There was no clear path to my dreams, and when it came time to move on, I stayed with SunTrust Bank yet again.

The new position, my fifth job in banking, was still under the marketing umbrella in SunTrust, and it allowed me the opportunity to do some writing. I was able to write copy for ads in local publications and speeches for some of the executives, which tapped into my creative side. My high school English teachers never would have guessed it, but I was really good at finding the words that sparked sales. It was empowering to know that I was able to do something the big shots couldn't do for themselves. For a while, the marketing job felt like a step in the right direction, even if it was nowhere near the top of the food chain at SunTrust. But deep down, I was *still* dissatisfied. I *still* knew that I was capable of more. I *still* felt that my potential was being overlooked.

I was still asleep at the wheel. I had just changed cars (and none of them were fancy).

I had a stable job, but I still had daydreams of a luxurious lifestyle, daydreams that I played so often in my mind's eye that they became almost more real than the mediocre life I was living. And why not? The mansion of my dreams was far more appealing than the reality of living with my mother in her 1,600-square-foot apartment.

Then one day, SunTrust eliminated my position. It was 2013, and after years of being stuck in a series of dead-end banking jobs,

I was upset. That's right. I was actually *upset* about losing a job that I knew would never get me to the life I wanted.

When you're asleep at the wheel, you just hope to stay on the road.

At that time, my marketing manager was one of my biggest supporters. She was one of the only people who saw that something in me, and she encouraged me to pursue more creative marketing work—not that there were many opportunities for creativity at SunTrust. She promised that she'd find me another position within the company, and she did. But it wasn't a life-changing opportunity, so I started looking at job listings online, just to see what else was out there.

Right away, a pattern emerged. Nearly every job that caught my eye—and *all* of the ones that fit my skills and experience—required an MBA. I could see the writing on the wall. I knew that my rise within the corporate world would be forever limited by my lack of a graduate degree. I needed to go back to school.

But make no mistake. I wasn't dreaming big. I wasn't hoping to score a CEO position or launch a hot new startup. When I lost my job, I was just looking to make myself more attractive to established companies so that I could land a slightly better job. That was the way people did things, right? All of the conventional wisdom said to be patient, to be satisfied with small steps.

Just get one or two rungs up the ladder, keep your head down, be grateful for what you get, and repeat until dead.

I was still asleep at the wheel, but I knew I needed a different driver's license if I was ever going to get anywhere.

WAKING UP

It took me a long time, but I finally gathered the nerve to leave SunTrust Bank. I accepted the severance package they offered and used the money to enroll in the MBA program. To pay my bills while I was in school, I took a job at Florida Community Bank. My new employer was a much smaller organization, just a fraction of the size of SunTrust, but it offered a lot of flexibility. I maneuvered myself into working remotely (which was rare before the 2020 COVID-19 pandemic) and created the perfect situation for pursuing my MBA. It wasn't demanding work, and I set my own schedule. For the first time in my life, I felt like I had at least some control.

But of course, it was still banking. I was still clinging to the only thing I knew, white-knuckling the steering wheel with both hands out of a fear of change and a lack of confidence. I still wasn't taking charge of my own destiny. I wasn't taking risks. I wasn't going after what I truly wanted: to show the world my talent, creativity, and capabilities. To be independent and rich. I was still moving forward with the idea of making myself more attractive to a corporate overlord.

When I entered the MBA program at Florida Atlantic University, I saw immediately that it wasn't exactly a hive of entrepreneurial spirit. This was not Harvard or Stanford. There were no kids starting dot coms in their dorm rooms. This was FAU, a state school in Boca where middle-aged folks were trying to open a hatch so that they could continue climbing the career ladder.

But one of my classes planted a seed.

About halfway through my graduate work, I took a course that included a unit on recurring revenue models in business. The concept immediately clicked with me: a subscription business that brought in steady money every month and didn't take much capital to launch was actually something I could do. That day in class started the wheels turning for me. I saw the huge potential of these types of businesses, and I started brainstorming. I started becoming more aware of the entrepreneurial world, of the tremendous upside of this type of business.

I also started reading quite a bit. I tore through everything from self-help to business books. I was seeking the advice that I had never received in my personal life, the wisdom that I never got from a mentor.

And I started to find it. One book in particular—*The 4-Hour Workweek* by Timothy Ferriss—stuck in my mind. I discovered authors who challenged the conventional notions of climbing a corporate ladder, and I began to view my career in a whole different way.

I was turning a corner. I realized that **taking risks *can* pay off, and that risk-takers were rewarded all the time.** Every day, someone leaves the nest, spreads their wings, and starts something of their own. I learned they don't always soar—but they don't always crash, either.

I always believed that I was smart and capable enough, and that if other people could only see that, I'd finally get to be successful. I had been waiting for my bosses to recognize my potential. But halfway through my MBA program, a new realization finally hit me: If I was going to be my own boss, *I* was the one who needed to believe in my talents.

I had always been going through the motions, wanting to change my life but not making any concrete moves to do anything about it. But I could feel that changing now. My mindset was shifting. I was ready to be proactive. I was ready to take the first steps toward what I really wanted. I was ready to actually *do* something.

My confidence was peeking from behind the curtain. It was almost time.

I just needed the right idea.

WIDE AWAKE

Once my mindset shifted and I realized I controlled my own destiny, I started seeing the world differently.

I looked at everything as a potential business.

Instead of looking at Uber drivers as poor suckers who had to haul the rest of us home from bars, I saw them as one-person businesses. Businesses with flexibility and freedom. I signed up to try it.

The experiment ended abruptly when a rider vomited all over the backseat of my Honda Accord, but I kept trying things. I kept brainstorming. I kept experimenting.

When I saw that pickleball was gaining popularity in South Florida, I didn't just see it as a weird fad. I saw it as another opportunity. I snagged a website name and started brain-storming how I might launch an online store devoted to pick-leball gear.

That idea didn't pan out either, but that wasn't the point. The point was that I was finally *seeing the opportunities around me*. I was looking for situations that would allow me to be my own boss. I was brainstorming ways to jump off the corporate tread-mill. Every single day, I ruminated on what kind of business I could start. My eyes and ears were open.

For some of us, starting a business is less like a lightbulb coming on and more like a snowball gaining momentum. That momen-tum I was creating—by reading, brainstorming, and exploring ideas—was taking me somewhere. I wasn't sure where it would lead, but I was up for the journey. I had no idea what business idea would ultimately win out as the perfect fit for me, but I was suddenly paying attention.

After years of being asleep at the wheel, I was finally wide awake.

MAYBE YOU CAN RELATE

Have you ever felt paranoid about losing a job that you didn't even like?

You're not the only one. I've been there. I get you. I have also held onto a job, constantly afraid that I'd get the axe. Clinging to a situation even though I was unhappy.

But you should know: it doesn't have to be that way forever.

It's possible to shift your mindset and set a new course. I'm not saying you have to start a business like I did. You could change direction within the corporate world. If you're a freelancer, you could find different clients or offer a new service. The particulars aren't important. What's important is to know that it's possible to open your field of vision. You get to wake up, look up from the boring task in front of you, and start to see the opportunities that are all around.

There *is* a way to get on a different path. There *is* a way to pursue that life you really want.

I found a way to get on that path. And if I found a way to do it, despite clinical depression and anxiety, despite going through a divorce, despite having no mentor in my life, then you can, too.

You don't need an MBA. You don't need to be rich already. You just need to tune out the noise.

As you wake up and start to explore new opportunities, you'll encounter some distractions. The first distraction will come from within—a little voice telling you that you shouldn't try something new. That's just a lack of confidence. I felt the same thing. It will take some practice, but it's something that you can overcome.

There will also be external distractions. This kind of interference is even more dangerous because it often comes from your friends or family, and might be *disguised as advice*.

You'll have to tune out the negative reactions you'll get when you announce that you're thinking of making a career change. The "advice" from some folks will reflect their own fears more than what you should do with *your* life. You might even encounter some people who don't want you to succeed at all, whether it's because they think you don't actually deserve it or because of a deep-seated insecurity that you'll become more successful than they are.

In the end, you'll just have to ignore the voices that tell you that you're just not smart or talented or creative or good enough to go against the grain and chart your own course.

When I stopped clinging to the jobs that didn't fulfill me and began looking for a way to seize my potential, I started an exciting new chapter in my life.

I still had a chip on my shoulder, and I still battled anxiety and depression, but I knew how to channel those feelings into something positive.

I knew the power of a healthy obsession.

KEY TAKEAWAYS

- **Learn** how to recognize when something is holding you back, whether that's your current position, your mental health, or even the people who are around you. Recognizing that there's a problem (and admitting to yourself that things need to change) is half the battle.

- **Reflect** on your current mindset: is it one of growth or of hindrance? You are in control of your life and have the power to shift gears from asleep at the wheel to driving in a new, fulfilling direction.

- **Act** by taking the necessary steps to improve your situation. For me, it was leaving the job that I hated, ending a marriage that wasn't working, and going back to school so I could pursue positions that better suited my creativity (not knowing the program would unlock my business idea). What does that look like for you? Whether it's a significant life change or a simple shift in mindset, taking action is critical.

CHAPTER 2

A HEALTHY OBSESSION

O nly eight minutes left. Damn it. I needed more time. Each tick of the clock over the door seemed to seal my fate.

"Quiero, quieres, quiere."

Out of the corner of my eye, I could see Zach signaling to the other boys.

Shit. It was definitely on.

"Queremos, queréis, quieren."

He glanced my way, and I quickly looked down at my desk. *Shit, shit, shit.* The anxiety welled up from my stomach and crept into my neck and shoulders. I started to feel lightheaded. The room suddenly felt ten degrees warmer.

"Can anyone use it in a sentence?"

I measured the distance to the door. Too far. When the bell rang, I'd have to walk right past them and…six minutes.

"C'mon, guys. You know this one. 'To want.'"

There were five of them and just one of me. Zach and his minions. They were all pretending to take notes, but they didn't fool me. If I didn't get out of there before the end of class, it would be *adios, muchacho* for me. They definitely had it in for me.

I had to find a way out.

"Anyone? Anyone?"

I raised my hand.

"Yes? Jonathan?"

"Quiero ir, um…a la…oficina," I said. I raised my eyebrows at the teacher, hoping she'd catch my drift.

"Good, Jonathan. That's…:

"Quiero *ir* a la *oficina*," I repeated. I tried to give her a wink, but it came off as an awkward blink. I wasn't very smooth back in ninth grade.

"Yes, you said that. But let's not always go to the *yo* form, okay? Can you give me one with 'they'?"

"Yeah, um…" I looked at my notes. "Quieren…" I desperately flipped through the glossary in the back of my text. *To kill, to kill…* "Quieren matarme!" I blurted out.

The teacher laughed. "A bit dark, but okay."

I motioned with my head toward the pack of boys on the other side of the room. "Ellos," I said.

"Thank you, Jonathan. Now let's try another stem-changer: dormir. Can anyone give me…"

Shit. She didn't get it. My heart pounded so hard I could hear it in my ears.

Four minutes.

I was running out of options. I turned to a fresh page in my note-book and stealthily slid it off the desk and into my lap where no one could see it. Then I slowly, carefully wrote an S.O.S. note.

"Miss Ritter, I'm about to get jumped after class. Can I leave early and go to the office so that I don't get my head kicked in? Thanks, Jonathan."

Now I just needed to get her the note.

———

At certain points in my life, my most intense bouts of anxiety took the form of paranoia. I was sure that people were plotting against me. I would imagine some catastrophe, and once I started thinking about it, I couldn't shake the thought. Even when it made me nervous or afraid, I kept right on thinking about it, creating a series of more and more awful variations on the theme.

I knew that there was something different about me. Other kids didn't get stuck in a thought loop about all the worst-case scenarios their imaginations came up with. They were happy and normal. But it was sometimes impossible for me to dismiss my paranoia and move on to lighter thoughts. I would rumi-nate on a single, terrifying idea, spinning in tight circles, unable to break free.

After a few of these incidents in my youth, my mother tried to get me the help I needed, and I was prescribed medication to control my anxiety and depression. I finished high school, earned a college degree, and began a career in banking. But in the background, just beneath the surface, there was a constant tension. A low, persistent drumbeat of submerged anxiety and depression. I controlled it enough to function, and I thought that I had it under control. After all, I was holding down a job, bringing home a paycheck, and going through the motions of everyday life.

But I would soon learn that my issues weren't really under control at all.

NOT THE HOLLYWOOD VERSION

It may not be sexy, but I'm going to tell you the real story.

Instead of painting a Hollywood version of a mental hospital, complete with a Jack Nicholson character and an evil nurse, I'm going to be completely honest—*I really don't remember much.*

That's what electroconvulsive therapy does to you.

I don't remember the faces of people at the hospital. Not the doctors, not the nurses, not the other patients. I don't even remember exactly how long I was there. *A week? Ten days?* I vaguely recall attending meetings, so I assume there was some kind of group therapy. I know I had a roommate, but I have no idea who it was. I have a faint memory of a couple of muscular guys in scrubs who brought us our food in the dining area. I remember thinking they could handle anyone who became agitated, if the need arose.

I remember locked doors. I may have checked myself into the hospital voluntarily, but I would not be released until the doctors were convinced I was no longer a danger to myself.

One of the side effects of electroconvulsive therapy is that it does a number on your memory. You can lose memories from the days and weeks surrounding the treatment, and sometimes even events that occurred before starting the procedure. So my days at the mental hospital are a blur. Unfortunately, I remember the events that led to my hospitalization all too clearly.

Those are the memories that I wish had been erased.

I was twenty-nine years old, with a wife and baby, and we had recently moved into my mother's spare bedroom back in Boca Raton. Things weren't going well.

I was married, but I didn't want to be married. I was a father, but I didn't feel ready to be a father. I had a job, but it wasn't going anywhere.

I had gotten married young, before I had the maturity to know what I wanted in life, so I had paired off with someone who wasn't right for me. And although I love my son with all my heart, and he's now the most important thing in my life, at the time, being a father just made me feel more anxious. I didn't know how to control all that despair and fear and be a dad at the same time.

That old tendency to ruminate began to kick in. Just as I did as a teen, I started to grind away on the same idea for hours on end. I ruminated on my stagnant life and how little it resembled the lives of everyone around me. My high school classmates all seemed to have it figured out—including some of the people who had made fun of me in my childhood, who were now living their best lives, bragging about their promotions on Facebook and blowing up Instagram with photos of their new houses and fancy vacations.

Meanwhile, I was almost thirty, and living with my mother again. I didn't like my job. I didn't like people I was working with. I was trudging along with no real plan, and no energy to try to come up with something better.

I put the wheels in motion for a divorce, but it didn't help my outlook. Even if I got out of my unhappy marriage, I was convinced that no woman would ever want to date me. Who would want a middle management dope who was twenty pounds overweight and sliding into middle age with nothing to show for it? I felt trapped. And sad. It was hard to get out of bed in the morning. It was hard to go to work.

It was hard to see the point of anything at all.

I went from doctor to doctor, psychiatrist to psychiatrist, hoping that adjusting my medications would continue to keep me functional. But I wasn't getting any better. I was so out of control that I started obsessing about my own state of mind. I incessantly researched depression, scouring the internet for symptoms, meds, side effects, and everything else. I read message boards for hours, investigating what others had experienced under various treatments. I would sit at my desk, bathed in the pale blue light of my laptop, scrolling through other people's misery. But my bleary-eyed research didn't bring me comfort. Instead of connecting me with a community, it left me feeling more alone than ever.

I've always known that I had an obsessive mind. That year I learned what my obsessive mind does when it has nothing to focus on: *it turns on itself.* I obsessed about obsessing. My depression depressed me. Thinking about my anxiety made me anxious. I dove into my own misery, overthinking and over-analyzing. None of my searching helped. It only worsened my despair. I was like that mythical snake that eats its own tail, inch by inch, until nothing is left.

I wanted it all to stop.

My ruminations turned darker. I saw myself jumping off of a building. Buying a gun. Ending my pain.

Thankfully, I found the courage to admit to a new psychiatrist that I was having suicidal thoughts. I confessed that I had even imagined specific ways of hurting myself. The psychiatrist nodded, took notes, then immediately arranged for my hospitalization. My depression had progressed to the point that the only goal now was to prevent me from self-harm.

Words like *suicidal ideation* and *self-harm* are medical terms. That's how all the doctors would describe what was happening to me, and that's all part of my official diagnosis. But these words also feel like euphemisms, polite ways of describing something that had so much power over me that I wasn't sure I'd survive it.

Sometimes I'm still not entirely sure how I did.

A few months after my hospitalization, the ongoing electroconvulsive therapy seemed to be working. It had pulled me out of the vicious spiral in which I had been trapped. I was still prone to a certain amount of anxiety and depression, and I think I always will be, but at least the depression was no longer calling the shots.

I had recovered enough to start making a few changes in my life. I followed through with the divorce, I took on a more creative role at work, and though I still had obsessive tendencies, I began to look for a positive outlet for my nervous energy and runaway thoughts.

I finally understood that I would always tend to obsess, so I needed to obsess on something *beneficial*, not self-destructive.

THE BRIDGE

I've faced plenty of mental challenges on my road to success. From the frustrating stagnation of dead-end jobs and a floundering marriage to the clinical depression and anxiety that almost ended me, I've had to get past some serious psychological hurdles along the way. Maybe that's why, after my hospitalization, I looked for an activity that would allow me to turn off my brain and push my body for a change. I wanted a *physical* test. And, *boy*, did I find one—the mother of all physical tests.

Mile fifteen of the New York City Marathon on the Queensboro Bridge.

When I entered the New York Marathon in 2010, I felt confident and prepared. I'd been training for a couple of years to work up to an event like this one, evolving from a casual (and very out of shape) jogger at first, to running 5K and 10K races with the goal of optimizing my performance, to completing half-marathons in the best shape of my life. I arrived at the starting point armed with a six-pack that would make superhero actors sweat and miles of practice under the soles of my sneakers. When the race began, the atmosphere was amazing. Thousands of fans lined the streets, cheering wildly and urging us on. It felt more like a block party than an athletic event. The energy carried me. I was cranking out the miles and cruising with confidence.

But when I hit the Queensboro Bridge, everything changed. No spectators are allowed on the bridge, so the raucous cheers faded behind me, and soon all I could hear were the footsteps of the other runners. Even the sunlight was dampened—we were running on the bridge's lower deck. I tried to hold my pace, but the incline of the bridge started to bite into me. Even though there's only a 3 to 4 percent grade to the bridge as it crosses the East River, that gentle slope seems to go on forever. The bridge is well over a mile long, and you run uphill for at least two-thirds of a mile. For someone who did most of their training in Florida, the flattest state in the country, the slow ascent was grueling.

My legs—the same legs that had been churning out miles like pistons—suddenly felt sluggish. My seven-ounce Nikes started to feel like concrete. That 3 percent grade felt like climbing the Swiss Alps.

That bridge almost broke me. Even the beating I took from Evan Engold in high school is nothing compared to the ass-kicking I got from that bridge.

My pace dropped off dramatically—there were even a couple of times that I had to put the brakes on completely and take time to breathe and regroup—but, despite my best efforts, I never got my legs back. I staggered to the finish line, nowhere near my time goal. I had looked for my limits and found them, and I was humbled by the experience. In hindsight, I've realized that a marathon is something that, regardless of how hard you train, you're never going to be fully prepared for. The human body is kind of not built to do that type of thing, especially if you aren't an athlete with that genetically optimized predisposition for running. Does that mean you can't try? Not at all, but it did mean that I probably should have expected more of an ass-kicking. But just so you understand what obsession looks like: The very next day I started training for the 2011 New York City Marathon.

———

I first tried running as a kid, mostly as a hobby. I even ran cross-country for a year in high school. But as I got older and life got busier, I dropped the habit. Years later, when I was living in Washington, DC, I decided to start running again, in part to help me cope with the stress of a rocky marriage and a newborn baby. But it was still a hobby.

It wasn't until after my hospitalization and divorce that my relationship with running became a full-blown obsession. I started slowly at first but worked my way up to tougher and tougher challenges. I reconnected with an old fraternity brother from college, and we started pushing each other to train harder. We worked our way up to six or seven miles a day, fifty miles a week.

I started losing weight and feeling better about myself, which motivated me to train even harder. The running obsession began to filter into other parts of my life. I started watching what I ate, experimenting with vegetarian and vegan diets. I got more structured and disciplined with my daily schedule to fit more training into my day.

I finally had somewhere to put my focus.

With my history of anxiety and depression, it was never good for me to be without a project or activity to fill my empty hours and give me something to focus on. I needed an outlet to channel my thoughts so that my ruminations wouldn't drift toward depression or paranoia. In running, I had found an obsession that pushed me physically and was good for me in many ways. Besides losing weight and giving me discipline, running triggered the release of endorphins in my system, which reduced my anxiety. My new passion for running proved to be much healthier than my paranoid obsessions about high school classmates or my ruminations on how pathetic my life was.

I spent the next year, after my first flop at the Queensboro Bridge, channeling even more energy than before into improving my endurance. I poured hours upon hours into my goal of performance optimization and engaged my creativity in crafting a routine that would prepare me for my archnemesis. Scouring South Florida for points of elevation, I found that worthy opponents were the drawbridges that had been built over major bodies of water, those that could open to allow for the passing of massive cargo ships.

When the 2011 New York City Marathon finally arrived, I had a strategic action plan. When I reached the Queensboro Bridge, I had enough gas in the tank to make it up and over that lonely, brutal bridge. In the end, I finished with my best-ever marathon time of 3:36—roughly an eight-minute mile pace.

For the first time in my life, my obsessive thoughts actually *helped* me. I got my revenge on that bridge, and it opened my eyes to a whole new way of thinking about my brain's natural tendencies.

There was a mindfulness in this healthy obsession, as if I was able to unplug myself from the paranoia-fueled anxiety spirals and instead plug into a wholly consuming focus that led me toward the life I wanted to be living. I could stop thinking about everything that was wrong long enough to make the changes that would lead to more things going right.

OBSESSION ISN'T ALWAYS A BAD WORD

Conventional wisdom frequently warns against the unhealthy side of obsession, but the truth is that **obsession can improve your life as well.** For me, there is such a thing as a *healthy obsession.* When I find a beneficial activity to focus on, my obsessive tendencies actually *strengthen* me, both physically and mentally. Obsessing about the right activity helps me to break away from destructive mental cycles by giving me an external target to focus on.

Tackling a challenging project channels my mental energy into something outside of myself. I need a finish line to chase, a horizon to keep my eyes on, a goal in the real world that I can strive toward. For me, it's all about finding the right challenge and choosing the right goals.

Maybe you can relate. Even if you don't suffer from anxiety or depression, perhaps you can still see the advantage of a healthy obsession. Whether you're hoping to overcome low motivation, a lack of confidence, or the paralysis of indecision, a **healthy obsession thrusts you into a project so completely that you forget the obstacles** that had been holding you back.

Unfortunately, my running career came to an end because of an injury—a herniated disc in my back. I could still run, but I couldn't be as competitive as I had previously been. After four marathons, I decided to hang up the running shoes. Training for marathons taught me that a healthy obsession can be a positive force in my life, so I immediately began the search for a new outlet—a new healthy obsession.

HEALTHY OBSESSION:
AN ENTREPRENEUR'S SECRET WEAPON

Not convinced that obsession can be healthy or beneficial? Let's fast forward a bit so I can prove it to you. In my experience with SinglesSwag, I witnessed the awesome results that can come from getting something exactly right.

Early on, I was completely obsessed with slogans and taglines. I played endlessly with combinations of words, hoping to land on one magical phrase that would click with my target audience. I ruminated, tested taglines, and observed what was resonating. I obsessed over slogans until I landed on one that I thought might be pretty good: "Singles Swag: When you're the love of your own damn life."

It was perfect. In fact, that one phrase may very well have built the business. Over 100,000 customers bought my product based on that tagline, and to this day, it's still our all-time most effective line.

My *overthinking* is what led to that breakthrough. And today, now that we're spending over $10,000 a day on ads, we *still* try to overthink our marketing strategy. We continue to test, adjust, and endlessly tweak our messages. It's just good business. And while I have now handed off many of my responsibilities to my operational team, I still obsess over the company's messaging. I still personally write and design our email campaigns. With a 450,000-person email list, I'm determined to get each message just right. I obsess over subject lines, taglines, and heat maps that show the best places on a web page to get customer interaction.

Eventually, you'll be able to hire a bigger team and delegate some of your tasks. You'll get to step back from the madness and return to a more sane schedule. You may even have time to search for your next healthy obsession—maybe even another business. But when you're first getting started, your company will be just you, flying solo.

And your only employee will be your obsession.

AN OBSESSION THAT PAYS

If you find yourself grinding on the same catastrophic thoughts over and over, unable to move on or shift your mindset, you may have a tendency toward obsessive thoughts. You should be aware that, if not managed properly, those tendencies can be destabilizing. If your obsessions are accompanied by anxiety, depression, or suicidal thoughts, you should reach out to someone immediately.

You should get the professional help you need.

I'm not a doctor and I don't pretend to be one. But I know what works for me. And in my experience, with the mental struggles that I've faced, one of my most effective strategies—after getting the treatment I needed—was to find an outlet, a healthy challenge, that would allow me to obsess on a goal and keep my mind on productive tasks.

I'm not saying that a healthy obsession is a *cure*—you're still obsessing over *something*—but it is the key to gaining more control over your anxious or obsessive tendencies and channeling them for positive change. If you find yourself bound by anxiety, leading to decision paralysis, career stagnation, or the inability to achieve the goals you want to achieve, zoning in on a healthy obsession may be the solution.

Unhealthy obsession, negative self-talk, and toxic overthinking will likely keep you standing still. Overcoming adversity feels good.

It can be liberating to throw yourself into a big project with a big reward and let yourself obsess over it. You can allow your mind to grind on a problem. Unlike wallowing in depression, if you choose the right project, the problem you're grinding on will actually have a solution. Instead of turning in tiny circles, you'll be headed toward the finish line.

If you want success badly enough, you truly want to change your life, *and* you've found a project that's healthy, *then give yourself permission to obsess.* Let yourself overthink. Use your obsessive tendency—what you thought was a weakness—to energize you and inspire a new, healthier direction for your life.

When I conquered the Queensboro Bridge that second time around, I knew that I had harnessed the power of my obsessive nature. I knew that my ruminations could be aimed at pretty much any aspiration, and that I'd obsess until the goal was accomplished. And now that my back injury had forced me into an early retirement from marathons, I was shopping for a healthy new obsession.

I *wanted* something that would keep me up late. I *wanted* something that would occupy my thoughts every waking moment—something that would force me to bring my whole self to a new challenge.

But I didn't want just *any* new obsession. I didn't want a hobby. I wanted something that would do more than just get me in shape. I wanted an obsession that would change *everything*: my self-confidence, my career, and even my personal life. I wanted a new kind of race—a marathon in which reaching the finish line would mean changing my life forever.

I was ready. I was going to try something I had always wanted to pursue but had never had the courage to attempt.

I had a feeling that this obsession would be perfect. It had thousands of details that would need attention and dozens of new skills that I would have to acquire on the fly. I would have to write, design, solve problems, and take risks. And, unlike destructive obsessions (like doom scrolling news feeds or searching WebMD for rare cancers), working till the wee hours on this project could actually reward me.

The more I thought about it, the more excited I got. For the project I had in mind, obsession wouldn't just be helpful, it would be *required*.

I was going to start a business.

Now I just needed the right idea.

KEY TAKEAWAYS

- **Learn more about yourself.** What makes you excited? What makes you fall apart? How do you process new information? Understanding your strengths and shortcomings is very important on the road to not only bettering yourself but starting a life-changing business or revitalizing a stagnant career. It's with this understanding that you chart a path forward.

- **Reflect** on the weaknesses you discovered in your self-exploration. My obsessive tendencies were *toxic* when left to their own devices, leading me further and further into anxiety, paranoia, and depression. I knew I couldn't stop my brain from functioning the way it was designed—I had tried with medications over the years—so there had to be another way. Accept what you cannot change and focus intently on what you can control.

- **Act** by writing everything out, including what you've learned about yourself and the specific, actionable goals you want to achieve. Search for opportunities to channel your struggles and shortcomings into positive change. Find your healthy obsession.

CHAPTER 3

FROM IDEA
TO REALITY

It was another Saturday night on the couch, watching a '90s movie after putting my son to bed.

But I couldn't focus on the movie. My mind was still grinding away on possible business ideas. *Should I give Club Pickle another chance? Pickleball is taking off, and people will need the gear. But wouldn't I just be another sports retailer? Can't people get that stuff at Champs or Dick's?*

I missed one of my favorite lines in the movie. I checked the time: one in the morning. I should've been in bed. But I couldn't stop thinking about business ideas.

Maybe the graduation cap thing was better. People would love that, for sure. Especially the customization—having the logo or the school mascot printed right there on top. But there are the licensing fees. Getting the rights to the official logos would be big bucks. Where would I get that kind of cash?

The movie wasn't as good as I remembered. It felt dated now.

My mind turned back to subscription services, the business model we'd been studying in my MBA program. Recurring revenue— *that* was the way to go. They were everywhere, after all: fitness centers with monthly membership fees, cable and streaming services (like Netflix, Hulu, HBO Max), software as a service (SaaS) subscriptions and business-to-business (B2B) website services, apps on our phones and the "Subscribe and Save" options on Amazon, Wine of the Month Club, or even those boxes—like the case study in class—*what was it called?* Oh, yeah—Birchbox.

How many customers did they have, all billed on autopay? How many of those customers didn't even *keep track* of how many recurring revenue model businesses they were subscribed to? *Well played, Box People.* While boxes make up a small portion of the recurring revenue/subscription space and are relatively young in the industry, the barriers to entry are far lower than a lot of other businesses operating within the same model. All you really need to begin is a website—like many e-commerce companies. This is why there are hundreds of thousands of boxes: food, beauty, jewelry, men's, women's, kids', sports, toys, survival gear, fishing—the list is literally endless, and the market is now full of niche boxes for all kinds of interests. That part was attractive to me, but my ideas at the time just didn't fit that mold. Graduation cap of the month? *Who graduates every month?* Pickleball racquet of the month? No way.

I had to get my mind off of business. I checked my phone. It was the weekend, so everyone was posting on Facebook and Instagram, showing off their amazing lives. Couples enjoying a night out, partying on a boat, attending the grand opening of—*is that the new bar down the street from me? Damn. It looks cool. If only I could...*

No. I suppose not. I was on single-dad duty, and Jacob was only five years old.

I wasn't going anywhere.

The movie droned on. I looked at my phone again. All of those people out there on a Saturday night, having a blast, living their best lives. I couldn't take it. I tossed my phone aside.

You all suck.

I wasn't even dating anyone. I'd given it a shot after my divorce, of course, but nothing had worked out. I thought of my most recent relationship. I still cared about her, but she had just dumped me for someone richer. Someone who was going places. *Shit, thinking about it isn't helping.* I felt lonelier than ever. I missed having someone to watch movies with. Someone to go to dinner with. Or surprising each other with gifts "just because," even—or maybe especially—when there wasn't an occasion.

Cut it out, Jonathan. Stop feeling sorry for yourself. You're not the only one in America who's single and alone on a Saturday night. There are millions like you.

You're not the only one who hasn't gotten a gift in a while.

And then it all clicked into place.

Millions. Like me. Single. Hadn't gotten a gift. Subscriptions. Millions. Singles. Subscriptions. Gifts.

Holy shit.

I turned off the TV.

———

That night, SinglesSwag was born. Customers sign up to receive monthly packages, which include everything from organic beauty products to fashion accessories to artisan-crafted foods. It's for people who want to put smiles on their *own* faces rather than wait around for someone else to make them feel good. A surprise every month in the mail, all designed to make you feel great about yourself and your life—no partner required.

From the moment I had the brainstorm, I knew I was on to something big. That night, I stayed up for hours, scouring the internet to see if anyone else had already launched something similar. But the niche hadn't been filled, so I jumped on it. I started purchasing domain names: SinglesCrate, SinglesBox, and of course, SinglesSwag.

Over the next few days, I honed the concept. Although I'd been thinking of my own situation when I had the idea, I quickly learned that the consumers of subscription boxes were primarily women. So, I shifted the focus to that demographic. I then took the idea to one of the smartest women I know. Someone who would be honest with me. Someone who wouldn't stroke my ego or waste my time: my mom.

Thankfully, she gave it the thumbs-up. In fact, she was excited at the possibilities.

That was all the confirmation I needed.

From that moment on, I didn't hesitate or second-guess the concept. I worked on the idea day and night, thinking of everything I could possibly do to make the business a success. I gladly threw myself into the project. I was motivated. I was inspired.

I had found a new *healthy obsession*.

And for the first time in my life, my obsession could actually move me closer to what I'd always wanted. It could get me out of my career rut. It could take my mind off of my anxiety and depression. It could give me a new kind of challenge that I had never faced before.

And it could make me rich.

THE LEARNING CURVE

"It's for single women?"

"Yeah."

"And it makes them feel better about being single?"

"Well, kind of…" I said. At the time, I was still refining the pitch. Now, though? SinglesSwag has a well-defined answer to this question and a clear mission for anyone interested in what we do—right on our website.

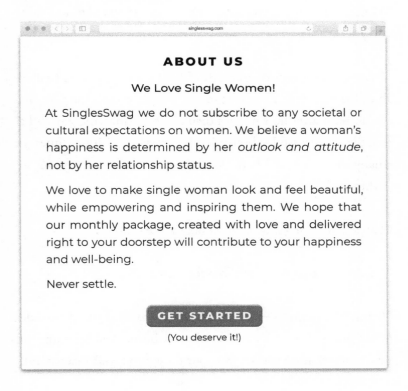

ABOUT US

We Love Single Women!

At SinglesSwag we do not subscribe to any societal or cultural expectations on women. We believe a woman's happiness is determined by her *outlook and attitude*, not by her relationship status.

We love to make single woman look and feel beautiful, while empowering and inspiring them. We hope that our monthly package, created with love and delivered right to your doorstep will contribute to your happiness and well-being.

Never settle.

GET STARTED

(You deserve it!)

"And you're a man?"

"Last I checked. But that's not really—"

"Can I ask you a sorta obvious question?" He sounded supremely annoyed by the whole conversation.

"Sure," I said, bracing myself.

"What the hell do you know about single women and how they feel?"

I was raised by one, I thought. But I held my tongue. I had called him for advice, so I couldn't much complain when he gave me some, no matter how much I disliked it. Besides, the guy had a relatively successful subscription box service, with ten times as many customers as I had. "Well, I mean, women are *people*, so I think—"

"You should bring a woman on board," he said.

"I just think that some of those feelings are universal. So—"

"Bring in a partner—a *woman* partner—to help you get inside their heads. Or else you'll crash and burn. And speaking of crashing, what do you know about these products? Beauty stuff, jewelry, all that."

"Well…"

"Have you ever done a subscription service?" he asked. He was on a roll now. He was starting to enjoy this. "What do you know about these boxes? Do you really know what the hell you're doing?"

"I'm a quick learner. I think I can—"

"Oh, wow. You're screwed."

———

It's true. I didn't know what I was doing. And almost everyone I went to for advice pointed this out. In fact, most of them told me that my lack of knowledge and experience would more or less guarantee my failure. But—and this is important—*I didn't let that stop me.*

I came from the world of financial services and marketing, and I didn't know jack about e-commerce, digital advertising, or women's lifestyle products. I had no experience with recurring revenue models. I had never subscribed to a gift box service in my life.

I was clueless.

But I also *knew* that I was clueless. So when I was getting SinglesSwag off the ground, I spent most of my time learning. I researched everything I didn't know, dedicating every waking hour to market research.

Don't get intimidated by the term *market research*. At that stage in the business, I was bootstrapping the whole venture, so "market research" didn't mean convening focus groups or conducting consumer surveys. I couldn't afford any of that. Research for me at that point consisted of two main activities: creating my own "subscription curriculum" with online resources and buying boxes from other companies.

MARKET RESEARCH:
A VALUABLE ENTREPRENEURIAL TOOL

Market research nowadays can take two forms: data mining and traditional. In data mining, massive amounts of data are aggregated to inform a company (or overall industry) of patterns in buying, using complex algorithms to sort, understand, and predict patterns and trends. Sounds like you need to be a mathematician or statistician, right? But you encounter it all the time! When Amazon tells you the items that other people typically buy when you put one item in your cart or when Netflix suggests new shows to you based on your watch history, that's data mining. Traditional market research, on the other hand, may include focus groups, surveys, and interviews, and is probably what most people imagine when they hear the term.

When you're bootstrapping a new venture, you may find that market research doesn't look like either of these, and that's okay. Even if you do not have the budget to conduct focus groups or engage in data mining to compile massive amounts of data, there is still a lot you can do and most of it is *free*.

Market Research Action Items

Study the Competition
- Website Review
    - How many pages are there? How many clicks to get to checkout?
    - How simple is it to place an order?
    - What's their email collection strategy?
    - What type of imagery and messaging do they showcase?
- Analyze Social Media Accounts and Strategy
    - How often are they posting? What content are they posting?
    - Are they actively engaging with their audience on posts? How?
    - Are they partnering with brands and influencers?
    - Is there a face of the brand?

- Order Their Product
  - How long does it take to arrive?
  - What type of post-purchase communication do you receive?
  - What do you think of the packaging? The product(s) itself?
  - Do they communicate a brand voice?
- Engage with Their Customer Service Team
  - Initiate a return to see how they handle it.
  - How long does it take them to respond?
  - Do they accept inquiries on multiple channels (email, social, phone, etc.)?
  - How do they make you feel about being a customer?

I hit the internet hard to study blogs, websites, and tutorials by others who had found success with their own subscription box businesses. Call it the subscription school of hard knocks. I read everything I could about creating a subscription business plan, packing and delivery logistics, acquiring customers, preparing for launch, and every other topic they offered. I put together a basic blueprint for the business this way, but I also wanted to know what worked and what didn't in the *real world*.

So, I ordered boxes from all the most successful companies.

I tried to immerse myself so that I could really get to know the business. I worked my way through piles of boxes, studying what products my competitors were including, how the items were presented, what notes or letters they included, and even the look and feel of the boxes themselves.

I knew I had to be thoughtful about every detail. I analyzed how each company differentiated itself, how they leveraged their social media assets, and how they acquired customers. And, knowing that my pricing could make or break my business, I investigated which boxes kept their subscribers the longest and what pricing strategy they used to achieve that longevity. This is one of the *most important* parts of creating and scaling a recurring revenue business. Massive corporations like Netflix or LA Fitness have a seemingly bottomless pit of money that they can pour into advertising. Their cost of acquisition is high, but the volume of customers they have and the longevity of those memberships make up for it. Smaller businesses, like SinglesSwag, couldn't play the same game. I had to be smart about my marketing and I had to do it at a very low cost with a high return on lengthy subscriptions.

This was all part of a structured pre-launch that I knew I had to get right for my business to go anywhere. In the recurring revenue business, it's very hard to raise prices. If you do, you'll just end up alienating loyal customers and they'll cancel on you—the kiss of death in a business that's all about *keeping* subscribers for as long as possible. I had to make sure I understood everything about the economic model up front, both how it would work at first and how it could scale at different subscriber thresholds. Getting the price right was just one of the many things I treated as a healthy obsession while I taught myself the ropes.

Everything I know about the box business, I had to go out and learn on my own. It just proves that when **it comes to entrepreneurialism,** *not knowing* **is no excuse.** The information is available, you just have to go get it. What's more, there's no harm in emulating what other companies are doing right. What's that old saying—good artists borrow, great artists steal? Yeah, apply that here. Or, if it sounds better, don't reinvent the wheel.

I wasn't afraid to learn from the companies that were already thriving in the marketplace. I wasn't shy about picking up great tricks from my competition. But the more I studied them, the more I realized that I was missing something they all had. Something that even the online subscription school claimed was one of the secrets to success. It was the key to getting traffic to my website. It was the formula for landing new customers.

I needed a following.

THUMB WARRIOR

Like. Like. Like. Like. Like. Like.

I was determined to prove that I could start my own subscription business, despite what advisors had so confidently assured me. I wanted to show that it could be done without prior experience or fat-cat investors.

Like. Like. Like. Like. Like. Like.

But I knew that if I wanted to get the attention of customers, I needed a social media audience. So, I read articles on how to cultivate a following on Instagram, the hottest app at the time (this was before TikTok shook things up). Instagram wasn't just added exposure for subscription box businesses. It was the foundation of many of the leading companies and gave them credibility.

Like. Like. Like. Like. Like. Like.

I started an Instagram account for SinglesSwag and immediately started posting. And I posted a lot—memes, photos, and product shots, labeling each one with relevant hashtags: #singles, #singleAF, #selflove, #treatyourself, and so on.

Like. Like. Like. Like. Like. Like.

I had also learned through my research that for every hundred photos you liked within a relevant hashtag category, you could count on roughly ten people to follow you, as long as you're posting material consistently. So, of course, I *obsessed* about that. I'd sit around "liking" relevant content all day and night. I felt like a digital coal miner, slogging away until my eyes could barely focus.

Like. Like. Like. I'm gonna need fucking thumb surgery after this. Like. Like. Like.

Thankfully, my day job at the time wasn't demanding. It was a remote job that only required an in-person meeting every month or two. The few hours a day that I had to clock in for that gig could be completed at home or even a Starbucks, if I needed a change of pace.

How many followers now? Okay, getting there. Like. Like. Like.

The foundation of my business was just me, all alone, liking tens of thousands of photos on Instagram and trying to think up clever posts. Of course, when you're staying up till three in the morning, being clever is harder than it sounds. But one thing was working well: since I had narrowed my focus to only single *women*, I didn't have to worry about what men thought of my material. It allowed me to be much more targeted with my memes, quotes, and offerings, and it helped me connect with followers.

And it was working. Engaging with my potential customers on Instagram got them to like SinglesSwag, and over a two-month period I jumped from the first one hundred followers to over five thousand. This was an *engaged* audience, too, so they were a built-in group to market to directly once we began selling boxes and generating revenue. *Boom!* My low-cost strategy without a major investment or devoted marketing team was going off even better than expected. I also set up a free landing page for email collection, so we let people know the minute we started selling boxes.

Like. Like. Like. Like. Like. Like.

My obsessive traits were a benefit in this phase of the business. I "liked" while eating dinner, "liked" while brushing my teeth, and even "liked" while I peed.

Like. Like. Like. [Flush] *Like. Like. Like.*

I started to see it as a test—a challenge to see if I wanted it badly enough. And I rose to the challenge, fueled in part by a desire to change my life, but also to prove to the naysayers that I really could accomplish something that they swore couldn't be done.

Like. Like. Like. Li—

"Try again later."

The message popped up on Instagram during one of my marathon sessions. I couldn't get back to the feed. *Wha—?*

Try again later? I looked again to read the small print below: "We restrict certain activity to protect our community. Tell us if you think we made a mistake." I suddenly couldn't access my account. I couldn't post, like, or interact with my growing audience. I was completely locked out. And then I realized.

Instagram thinks I'm a bot.

BUILDING AN ENGAGED AUDIENCE

When developing your business idea, one of the most important things you can do is develop and connect with your target audience *before* you launch. This will give you an immediate group of engaged consumers to market to and lean on for those all-important initial sales to begin building your business.

I relied on Instagram to build that community, and while many of the techniques I used could still work today, social media platforms and practices change fast. For the most up-to-date advice on how to structure the pre-launch phase of your business, including how to build your brand, visit *JonathanBeskin.com*.

IT'S NOT HARVARD, IT'S HUSTLE

If you're launching a new venture, the beginning is often the most exciting part. Let that energy drive you forward. You'll need it for all of the homework you have ahead of you. That homework, along with some tenacity, is the only thing standing between you and a successful business.

And to those of you who think I had an advantage because I studied finance in undergraduate school and then got an MBA? Nope. That had surprisingly little to do with my success.

Seriously—it didn't really help.

At the classes I attended, my professors presented business in a very *theoretical* way. Even when we were discussing actual case studies, we approached them like they were bugs under a microscope. We didn't go out into the field to see warehouses or factories or the home of someone starting a business out of their garage. And a lot of these online companies don't show up in textbooks because these types of businesses are brand new. They've sprung up in the last few years in response to a growing trend. Business school curricula just can't keep up with what's hot in the real world.

So you don't need an Ivy League education. Trust me.

You're better off with an eagerness to soak up all the knowledge you can along the way. I successfully launched and scaled my business with nothing but obsession and a bit of hustle.

Most of the information you'll need is available on the internet, and almost all of it is free. You just need to approach it with positivity. Don't assume that you *can't* do something just because you don't know *how* to do it. Don't assume that you can't figure out how to do Facebook ads just because you've never done one. I didn't know the first thing about Facebook ads, but I figured it out. I'm no genius, but I managed to scale my Facebook advertising from $20 a day to over $10,000 a day in three years. (SinglesSwag has now spent around $15 million on Facebook ads to date.) Too many people default to, "if I don't know it, I'm not going to be able to learn it," but that's simply not true.

Besides an eagerness to learn, you'll need a willingness to make sacrifices. And I don't mean *monetary* sacrifices. The notion that you'll lose money for the first few years of business is a common misconception. It doesn't apply to certain sectors. I never went into debt to launch my online business. At every step of building SinglesSwag, the company turned a profit. Even the first month was profitable.

What you will have to sacrifice is *time*.

I was willing to sacrifice all of my free time to build my business. Instead of watching movies, I was watching how-to videos on YouTube. Instead of going out on the nights I didn't have my son, I was at home reading online articles. I wasn't binging Netflix, taking vacations, or browsing dating apps. I put my personal life on hold and invested my time in this goal.

It will be tedious to learn everything you need to learn. It will take commitment. You'll have to throw yourself into the project. And it may take a while to master some of the new skills you need, but *all of the necessary info is out there waiting for you.* Within five minutes, you can locate all of the information you'll need to learn Facebook and Google ads. Sure, it will take some time to get *good* at digital advertising, but nothing's stopping you from getting started.

And there are no barriers to entry for most online businesses. Build-your-own-website companies will take money from anyone. They don't ask for qualifications when you sign up for services. Google Ads won't work exclusively with experienced advertisers. As long as you pay, you can play. It doesn't matter to them if you're an ad agency with thirty years of experience or someone who's just starting out. That door is wide open to everyone.

Finally, just as you shouldn't convince *yourself* that you can't do something, you shouldn't let others convince you that you can't succeed, either. While there are some encouraging entrepreneurs out there who will try to be supportive, there are also plenty of know-it-alls who will act more like gatekeepers than allies. Like the people in the gated communities of Boca Raton, these entrepreneurs don't want their neighborhoods getting too crowded by letting just anyone in. They will pretend to be supportive by giving you some "tough love" or "difficult truths that you need to hear," but what they really want is to discourage you.

Anyone who says you can't start a business either doesn't know what they're talking about or is just guarding their territory.

Once you've found a goal that gets you inspired, go for it. And regardless of whether you reach the goal, it can still be a healthy exercise. You'll gain a ton of new expertise, you'll master new skills, and you'll have a healthy obsession to occupy your mind.

DON'T LET THE CROWD SCARE YOU

Let's imagine that you just came up with a great idea for a business. You're thrilled. Your adrenaline is surging. This will be your big break. You're sure of it. You run to your computer to see what similar businesses are out there and...

Several companies are already doing what you wanted to do. They beat you to it. They're out there now, selling millions of products to the customers you were hoping to land. You slump down in your chair, depressed.

But why are you afraid of a crowded market? Because someone told you that you needed a completely original idea? Or someone told you that you should avoid competition?

The need for a 100-percent-original unicorn of an idea is largely a myth. And the idea that you shouldn't get into markets with many competitors is partially a myth. One of the warnings I heard when I was getting ready to launch SinglesSwag was,

"How are you going to grow? There are big companies already doing this, and they're shipping *millions* of boxes a year! How are you, some nobody with no money, going to stand out in that crowd against those heavy hitters?"

Of course, you probably *should* avoid a crowded market if competitors are all fighting over a dwindling base of consumers in a fading trend. But I think a crowded space is the best place to be if it's also *crowded with customers* and still *growing*. Early in my research on box subscription services, I discovered that the average person who subscribes to a subscription box actually subscribes to 3.1 subscription boxes. People who have an affinity for the monthly box model tend to buy more than one.

So I realized this wasn't a case of straight competition. It wasn't a zero-sum game. A customer could subscribe to one of the big, established box services and still try mine as well. I also learned that you can make a product that customers like *better* than the existing options. You can win over customers and get them to switch over to your brand.

So don't be afraid of crowds. Would you rather open a business in a bustling market or in one of those deserted malls?

You can also *differentiate* yourself from others doing similar things. Sure, there were plenty of companies marketing subscription boxes to women when I entered the game, but I very specifically tailored my service to *single* women. And my brand just had a different vibe. In addition to humor and warmth, my brand had *attitude*.

For example, one of the benefits of my healthy obsession—which required me to spend hundreds of hours studying other people's email campaigns and language patterns—was that I became a lethal weapon when it came to email subject lines.

Subject Line: When You're the Love of Your Own
Damn Life
Subject Line: Your Ex Is A Tool 🔧
Subject Line: Annoyed At First Sight
Subject Line: Marry Me? Anyone?
Subject Line: Self-Love Is Not Cancelled
Subject Line: Cupid Rhymes With Stupid
Subject Line: Being Toxic Is Not Cute
Subject Line: Things Not To Do In 2023 (Your Ex)
Subject Line: Self-Care Is How You Take Your Power
Back
Subject Line: Commitment Issues
Subject Line: Day 481 Without Sex
Subject Line: Netflix and Avoid People
Subject Line: 1-800-HIS-LOSS
Subject Line: The GOAT Of Boxes

And when I say we had attitude, I mean it in every way, including an Instagram feed full of memes like the ones below:

There are plenty of myths out there that can dissuade you from starting a business, but the only truly important thing to consider before you launch your venture is this: do you have the *drive* to do it? Are you motivated enough to go out and learn what you don't know, build a following, and out-perform the established companies?

If you have the fire, the curiosity, and the willingness to take on competitors, you'll be fine.

Once you have those basics, you'll just need to *trust yourself and the idea* that you love so much. There will be moments that will test you, but you have to stick with it.

I faced one of those moments very early on. A pivotal moment in which I had to trust my intuition and hold tightly to my confidence in my idea. I had just announced my new business to my friends and family, and…

It didn't go as planned.

KEY TAKEAWAYS

- **Learn** all that you can about the industry you want to break into and the established companies that are doing what you want to do. Obtaining an MBA *helped* me for sure—and helped to inspire my winning idea—but a majority of my business lessons were learned well outside of the classroom. You don't need an Ivy League education to do this, you just need time.

- **Reflect** on the excitement you feel as you begin your new venture or new path and let that energy drive you forward. There may be moments where you feel overwhelmed and confused—that's *okay*! It takes time to become an expert in anything, but that drive you feel to do better for yourself and the people around you, to unlock your potential...that is something that can't be erased.

- **Act** by taking the first steps to turn your idea into reality. Secure website domains, establish legal entities, obtain social media handles, and start to research and learn. Get excited about your new venture and potentially your new healthy obsession.

CHAPTER 4

FEAR AND VULNERABILITY

Boca Raton, Florida, has some of the wealthiest gated communities in the entire nation, and as I approached middle school, I became more and more aware of the glaring differences between the haves and the have-nots.

My mother and I lived on her modest teacher salary, which in that world was considered one step above food stamps. It's not like I could carry around a copy of her tax return to prove them wrong, so I was stuck with the image they had of me. While some of the other kids could afford to throw lavish parties at country clubs or in the clubhouse of their wealthy enclaves, I was never invited. I was an outsider, one of the kids who just couldn't compete in the social circles of Boca Raton tweens.

But I had an ace up my sleeve: my bar mitzvah.

No matter what the kids at school thought of me now that things like designer clothes and the name of your fancy summer camp mattered, I knew that for at least one day, I would be the center of attention. There would be at least one gathering where I would be the star.

When the day arrived, I was nervous. The service was held in a large synagogue, and it was packed with friends and family. I couldn't wait to get through the religious part and move on to the party, where I would officially make my debut on the seventh grade social scene—and hopefully get a do-over on my status as *persona non grata*.

I got through my Torah portion just fine, if you don't count my voice cracking and my hands getting so sweaty, I had to wipe them on my pants. I was already daydreaming about some '90s dance moves I planned to unveil at the party. Things were finally going to go my way.

Unfortunately, the service wasn't over. We had yet to hear the blessings from family members, which were short speeches to celebrate the occasion. After a couple of other relatives, my dad took the mic to say a few words. He pulled a piece of paper from his jacket pocket, unfolded it, and cleared his throat.

And that's when everything went sideways.

Without even looking at me, my dad barreled ahead with his speech. There were no words of congratulations or any sense that he regretted the time he had missed with me. I don't think he even said my name.

What was the theme of this speech, which he had clearly taken the time to write down ahead of time? My mom.

In front of the rabbi and a packed temple, my father laid out his grievances in excruciating detail. He began with a general complaint about not being included in the planning of the bar mitzvah, which led to a general tirade about my mother shutting his family out of important events. He turned increasingly vitriolic, vindictive, and unhinged. He berated and belittled her. He clearly delighted in wounding her.

I don't think he cared a bit about how it all felt to *me*. Every word of the speech was about him: *his* anger, *his* grievances, *his* outrage.

The audience watched in stunned silence. I slid lower and lower in my chair, covering my hot face with my hands.

When his rant finally wound down and he surrendered the microphone, I peeked at my mom. She was shattered. And because I loved her so much, I felt every ounce of her pain on top of my own embarrassment.

I was ashamed.

Afterwards, when we all convened for the *oneg*, a brief festive gathering at the synagogue, my dad was still behaving rudely, and the rabbi had to ask him to leave. He strode through the door like a man perfectly accustomed to being kicked out of events, with his trademarked "life's a bitch and then you die" swagger. I had let myself hope that my bar mitzvah would be different. That it would be special. But deep down, I knew this was how my dad was. My whole life, he had gotten into road rage incidents and fights with waitresses and salesmen, always playing the part of supreme asshole.

I looked around at the other kids. They all stared at the food or out a convenient window, desperate to look anywhere but at me. Without a single set of eyes to latch onto for comfort, I stared at the floor. Maybe it was easier for everyone that way.

This was supposed to be my big day. My shining moment. My chance to finally be the star.

But he couldn't even let me have that.

———

Yes, my bar mitzvah was a dumpster fire. But my father's crazy, inappropriate behavior didn't start there. It started long before.

After my father got out of prison, he never returned to the family. Throughout my childhood, my interactions with him were limited to once-a-year visits, traveling to see him five states away.

As I approached adolescence, my dad tried to spend some more time with me in an effort to rekindle our relationship. But how do you rekindle something that never existed?

It didn't go well.

He would appear for surprise cameos, modeling the worst behavior imaginable. Even just taking me to lunch, he would drive like a maniac, swearing and flipping off other drivers in a violent rage. He was constantly getting into fights in public with no regard to how it would affect me as I watched.

He also subjected me to a nonstop litany of complaints about my mother. And while she never spoke ill of him, he didn't hesitate to try to poison my mind against her. He would then disappear again, leaving me to deal with the psychological fallout.

But none of the antics he pulled during his visits were as hurtful or harmful to me as the performance that he staged at my bar mitzvah. When he was finally kicked out of the oneg (which he had not been invited to), I admit that I felt an overwhelming sense of relief. The next day, when the full impact of the episode finally sank in, I sat in a car with a few other relatives, crying my eyes out.

My bar mitzvah was the first time in my life that I put myself out there. It was my first time speaking in front of an audience, my first time standing up in front of others and hoping for validation. What I got instead was humiliation, shame, and the understanding that no adult had stood up for me in the moment to try to stop it. The damage was deep and lasting. From that point on, I avoided any situation in which I could be subjected to public scrutiny or criticism.

I didn't want to take the risk of being embarrassed publicly. It was one of my biggest fears.

So, when I finally came up with a good business idea, one that I hoped could make a positive change in my life, I wasn't sure I could announce its launch.

THE DECISION

"Jonathan Beskin wants you to like a page on Facebook."

It was a straightforward message that would go out to all my friends, past coworkers, family, and acquaintances. Hundreds of people would receive it. All I had to do was click "send."

But I hesitated.

I opened a new window on my laptop and went over the SinglesSwag Facebook page one more time. The images were fine, the writing was solid, the new business proposition was clear. It was ready. I took a deep breath. All I had to do was click that little button.

All of my fears and insecurities took up residence in my index finger. It hovered over the keyboard for a moment, caught between my fear of opening myself up to public criticism and the excitement of finally launching my own venture. I looked around my living room. I didn't have a den or home office. Often, in order to get some work done, I had to go to a nearby Starbucks. I needed more space. I needed a new couch.

I needed a new life.

But my finger still hovered. *What if they all laughed at me? What if they think I'm an idiot?* Some of those same people who beat me up my whole life...*will they take shots at me for trying something new?* I felt completely vulnerable. It felt like I was about to give a speech—with no preparation—about quantum physics at halftime of the Super Bowl.

In the nude.

There was no way I could do this.

My insecurities were deafening. *Why am I torturing myself? This is never gonna work. SinglesSwag is never gonna go anywhere. I'm a complete failure. Fuck me.*

I looked around the room again and thought to myself: *what if I don't start this business? What will happen?* And I realized in that moment that if I didn't hit "send" and take the first step towards launching my own venture, what would happen was...absolutely nothing.

I hit "send."

—————

In my mind, one of two things would happen if I tried to start my own business. Either it would be met with skepticism and I'd be laughed at, or it would become a great success and change my entire life.

But real life isn't always so black and white. In the real world, the result of your actions is not as simple as your best- and worst-case scenarios would lead you to believe.

When I finally put my business out there, all my worst fears *did* come true.

But so did all my dreams.

A lot of people laughed at me. A lot of people ignored me. Many people assumed I would fail. Very few people wished me luck. But on the other hand, my life *did* change. And with a couple years of hard work, all my dreams *did* come true.

It wasn't one or the other. It was both.

When I invited all my connections to like and follow my social media pages, I had a specific objective: I needed some followers. I wanted my friends and colleagues to follow these SinglesSwag accounts so that when my first customers landed on these pages, there would already be some followers. If you invite a thousand friends to like a page, maybe fifty or so will actually do it. That's not a great return, but it's enough so that your business won't look like a scam. And it's definitely better than paying to get your first few followers.

In addition to the invite, I began posting on Facebook and Instagram about my launch. With great fanfare, I announced to my entire network that I was starting SinglesSwag, a subscription service for single women, and offered links to the official pages. But the name of my business, SinglesSwag, turned out to be somewhat polarizing. While a handful of folks loved it, many others were confused. They didn't bother to follow the links and read about SinglesSwag. They assumed I was starting a dating service or a porn site. Some people, reading that it was a "service for single women," let their imaginations run wild. They thought that perhaps I was peddling sex toys.

Ouch.

Other people assumed that my posts about SinglesSwag were some kind of elaborate joke. I remember one person reacting in the comment section with laughing emojis. This reaction hit me the hardest. It's as if that little yellow face was every kid in high school who ever made fun of my car or pointed at me the day after I got my ass kicked in the park.

The majority of the negative responses didn't have malicious intent—they were born out of honest confusion—but, after a lifetime of being conditioned to being treated with disrespect, I assumed the worst of many of the messages I received.

Some people weren't overtly negative, but weren't exactly supportive, either. Instead of wishing me luck, they asked questions dripping with doubt, such as: "What do you know about this business?" or "Isn't there a lot of competition?"

Whether people thought SinglesSwag was a sex business, a dating site, or an outright joke, the response was underwhelming.

And the few people who understood my idea had no problem letting me know that they doubted I could pull it off.

I was definitely fazed, but I wasn't defeated. I just needed to regroup and use the doubters as motivation.

I had to prove them wrong.

ADMIT IT—YOU CARE

Let's be honest: most of us care what other people think of us. We may pretend that once we reach adulthood, we no longer care as much, but we do. We want to feel understood. We want to receive positive feedback from others. We want to be respected.

It's natural to feel a prickle of doubt or the icy tingle of fear when you're preparing to launch a new project. It's nerve-racking to offer something for public consumption because that means it's also available for public criticism. And, if you grew up like I did, without some of the advantages the other kids had, you might already feel like an underdog. You might have a bit of an inferiority complex to begin with. So, it's hard to take a bold step with everyone watching. It's even harder to shake that feeling that you might get put back in your place. Maybe your worst fear isn't that the business won't succeed, but that people will think you're a fool.

So, should I tell you that everything will be okay? That everyone will love your idea? And that you'll get nothing but support, encouragement, and positivity?

That just isn't true.

There *will* be haters. And they'll let you know it. There will always be a certain percentage of people who think that your idea is silly or stupid. Part of your audience simply won't understand your idea. It won't connect with everyone, and some people will be rude about it. It's the dark side of human nature, I suppose, and it's unfortunate, but there will be people who just can't find it in themselves to hope that good things happen for you.

Not everyone will be rooting for you.

There will be moments when you just can't ignore those negative voices. There will be times when it starts to get to you. But you have to ask yourself: *do I want to change my life badly enough to endure a certain amount of negativity?*

On the one hand, you want to be your own boss, you want to be creative, and you want to try something new. Maybe you want freedom from the nine-to-five job that has made you feel trapped for years. What are those dreams worth to you? You may find that putting up with a few haters is well worth the potential reward of changing your life for the better.

Jonathan in the first SinglesSwag office.

In my own life, I eventually cared more about breaking out of my unfulfilling situation than I cared about potentially being embarrassed in front of others. I thought of SinglesSwag as a means to an end to achieve my goals. For the first time in my life, at thirty-five years old, I decided that those goals were more important to me than my fear of humiliation.

When you put a new idea out into the world, you can't control how people will react. If your idea doesn't resonate with someone and they rudely shoot you down, that person is just not part of your target audience. And because they are not in your target audience, don't spend your precious energy trying to change their mind about your venture. They wouldn't buy it anyway.

Instead, use your energy to empower *yourself.* Pour all of your efforts into making your idea the best it can be, and don't worry about converting the nonbelievers. Your belief in the idea is the most important thing, especially in the early stages. Take all of the intellectual and emotional energy you would use to confront negativity and use it to bolster your confidence in your idea instead. Every day, remind yourself what excited you about the original brainstorm. Then, use some of that energy to improve your product or service and to grow your audience.

For some of you, the negativity can actually *benefit* you. Some entrepreneurs take a pessimistic, cynical comment and let it piss them off. They then channel that anger into working harder. They're more motivated by the doubters; they're fired up to prove everyone wrong. They think, "You don't believe I can do this? Fuck you; watch me."

Negativity, if channeled properly, can fuel a healthy obsession and push you towards success.

THE DEAFENING SOUND OF SILENCE

In those early days of SinglesSwag, as I was navigating the psychological minefield of doubt, I held onto one dependable source of support: my mom.

My mom was the first to recognize the potential of my idea, and she was the one who consistently encouraged me throughout the journey. And while I sometimes took her enthusiasm with a grain of salt—she's my mom, she's *required* to root for me—that source of positivity helped me through some of my moments of doubt.

Her lone voice of support reminded me that there are people on my side, people who believe in me. I knew that, if all else failed, I could probably always count on at least some family members to be on my side. Although I have no siblings and my father wasn't a part of my life, I knew that my extended family—my aunts, uncles, and cousins—should be rooting for me in this new chapter of my life.

That's what family is for, right?

So, when my business started to gain steam and my entrepreneurial efforts gained traction in the national media, I was sure that some of my extended family would reach out to me with congratulations.

That did not happen.

Not one member of my extended family reached out to me with support. Even those who had let me cry on their shoulders after my disastrous bar mitzvah were oddly quiet. I'm not going to lie—I really could have used a pat on the back. After that rough beginning, I longed for a few messages of congratulations, even if it was something as simple as, "I heard your new project is going well! Great job!" I hoped for some validation after all of the time and effort I had thrown into the project.

All I got was silence.

I could've reached out to them, of course, but I couldn't think of a graceful way to do it. What would I say? "Hey! I'm successful now! How cool is that?"

Talk about cringe.

If you are fortunate enough to have a venture that takes off and becomes successful, there will still be disappointments. There will be people you assumed would be cheerleaders who, instead, just disappear. And you can't let it get you down.

Some people are just more comfortable with their old narrative of you. They prefer an outdated idea of you that they had already formed in their minds. They had already filed you as that struggling-artist friend or that crazy-ideas cousin. Maybe they liked it better when you came to them for advice, and they are now uncomfortable with the new dynamic.

Many of your friends and family sorted you into a mental file folder long ago. That file may have been labeled "dreamer" or even "failure." In my family, I suspect that some of my relatives developed deeply entrenched opinions of me back when I was struggling. To them, I will always be that kid who got in trouble in high school, who was sent to New Jersey to live with my aunt, who wasn't the best student, and who struggled with mental illness.

It can be difficult for some people to reassess their concept of you, especially if your new success doesn't fit their old idea of who you are.

You may also find that some of your close friends or family distance themselves from you out of a misplaced sense of competition. I have a cousin who has been trying to grow a business for thirty years. When my venture took off so quickly, she blocked me on social media and hasn't spoken to me since. If someone you know always believed that they would become successful before you did, it might be hard for them to congratulate you. They see the world as a zero-sum game, so if you're winning, they must be losing.

Their silence may be painful, but it's not about you.

Some of those friends and family members may eventually come around and reach out to you someday. They may gradually become more comfortable with this new version of you. But others will drift away forever.

It's a painful process, but you have to remember who you are doing this for. Remember why you started the project—to be successful, to change your life, to express your creativity, or to break free of the corporate world. It always feels good to get a pat on the back, but you have to remember that you had other reasons for launching your venture. Focus on your dream and what it will take to get there, then let go of anyone who doesn't support you. You can't let them take up the energy you need to make your idea a success.

FROM HATERS TO ADMIRERS

Not too long after launching, my company began to receive national recognition. When the pandemic hit, the company exploded to a whole new level. With everyone stuck at home, it seemed that every single woman in America wanted to buy herself a gift. SinglesSwag was growing in leaps and bounds, making the *Inc.* 5000 list of fastest-growing companies—in fact, SinglesSwag made the top 200 nationally, the top *ten* in Florida, and earned a full-page article in *Inc.* magazine.

Good things were happening. The business was featured on the *Today Show*, in *Cosmopolitan* magazine, and on *NBC News*. I was also invited to speak at the nation's largest conference for subscription and recurring revenue businesses. With the added press came a steadily growing phenomenon: I was suddenly picking up more admirers than haters. SingleSwag's social media accounts were officially "verified" by Instagram and Facebook, and our pages attracted over one and a half million real followers.

In other words, SinglesSwag was cultivating a community.

I had finally reached my target audience. I didn't have to worry about the haters because the admirers loved SinglesSwag. With the increased publicity, more people were finding us, connecting with us, and thanking us for what we were doing. So many people thanked me for fighting the misconception that single people aren't as happy as their married counterparts, that a single person can't live a fulfilled life. While many people subscribe simply because they like the products, there's also a large number of fans who appreciate that SinglesSwag offers something especially for them as opposed to the many companies out there marketing to married couples and families.

The beginning of any venture can be a trying time, especially as you deal with people who don't believe that you can succeed. But when your idea finally catches on, you might be pleasantly surprised by all of that positivity that you receive. You'll hear from the people who actually *get* your idea, who kick themselves for not thinking of it first, and who are rooting for you every step of the way. You will have all the fans that you wished you had early on.

Fast-forward to today, and instead of laughing emojis on Facebook, I regularly receive direct messages on Instagram or LinkedIn from total strangers who just want to reach out and genuinely congratulate me on what I've accomplished. Some of them even ask me for advice, which is, of course, flattering.

The lesson here is that there's a whole world of supporters out there. You have to find them, and they have to find you. That may take a while, but you'll never connect with those admirers if you never take the leap to begin with. Until you're willing to confront some of your fears and put yourself out there, you'll remain stuck in your current situation.

You may not ever fully conquer your fear of leaving yourself open to criticism. You might never get over your self-consciousness or anxiety about putting yourself out there. And that's okay. You don't have to. But you do need to learn to be vulnerable. You need to learn to put yourself in the line of fire of all the haters, cynics, and bullies of the world. Taking action may always be uncomfortable for you, but you can do it. The secret is to assess your goals and decide that they are more important to you than your fear of embarrassment or failure.

As you become more successful, it's possible that some people will hate you even more. But you'll also find validation and admiration that will make the whole journey worth it. That admiration and support may not come from where you had hoped or expected it to, but it's out there. And you'll only find it if you leave yourself open to it.

Once you've learned to take that scary leap and launch your ideas into the world, you're going to hear a lot of advice. Everyone's going to have an opinion about exactly how you should move forward with your venture. They'll tell you that there's one right way to do things, and they'll be quite sure of their expertise.

But most of the time, in my experience, they're full of shit.

KEY TAKEAWAYS

- **Learn** that actions speak louder than words, but the absence of either can be both deafening and devastating to your mental fortitude. However, once you find your target audience, in business or in life, the community that you can grow together can exceed your wildest expectations.

- **Reflect** on the fact that you do not need to be defined by your past or pigeonholed into a mediocre life— share your ideas with the world. It may not have been an incident as traumatic as my bar mitzvah. In fact, there may have been no major incident at all, but that feeling remains. Get to the bottom of it so you know how to walk yourself through when the feeling arises and come out on the other side.

- **Act** despite your fear. Lean into your doubts and insecurities, instead of hiding from them. Share your ideas with the world. Will everyone be a cheerleader for you and embrace your ideas? No. You can't control them or their thoughts or biases, but fortunately they can't control you or your success.

CHAPTER 5

NAYSAYERS
AND BAD ADVICE

Have you ever had one of those days when you could feel things turning around? When your whole body feels a bit lighter? When, after months of fighting for something, you could finally see a tiny glimpse of good news peeking around the corner?

That's how I felt one day near the end of 2016. This was going to be a great day. I could feel it.

I'd been grinding it out for months to get my subscription box business off the ground. I'd been scratching and clawing to get my number of subscribers up over 700. I spent long days and longer nights working social media and putting out fires as the growing pains of my company consumed almost every waking hour.

But then I had a stroke of luck. Because I'd taken the risk and announced my new venture on Facebook, and because my mom was doing her best to call attention to all my posts, one of her coworkers heard about SinglesSwag. As luck would have it, that coworker had a friend who was already well-established in the subscription box business—someone who had *ten times* as many customers as I did and who was willing to give me advice.

I was psyched—this was just the break I needed! I did some math and figured that this guy, Spencer, was pulling in over $140,000 in revenue each month. With some of his inside information and a few of his tricks of the trade, I could take my business to the next level. Maybe even pull in six figures in revenue a month, too!

I got my phone meeting, and I prepared diligently for the call. I wanted to show this Spencer guy that I was serious about wanting to succeed in his industry. I wrote out all the facts and figures for SinglesSwag: my advertising budget, acquisition cost of customers, monthly revenues, net profits, and the change in gross profit percentages with increasing volume. I included not only the average cost of a month's products, but also the cost of its component parts—down to the fancy tissue paper that frames the products in each box.

Maybe it was overkill, but I wanted to provide every single bit of info that would help *him* help *me*.

PER-UNIT ECONOMICS

	Monthly	Annually		2021 actuals
Monthly price	$40			
# of Months	6.11			
LTV	$180.00	100.00%		$12,297
CPA	($57.50)	-31.94%		
COGS Total	($39.72)	-22.06%	$6.50	14.47%
Shipping Total	($48.88)	-27.16%	$8.00	31.35%
Logistics Total	($10.08)	-5.60%	$1.65	Incl. above
CSR	($0.10)	-0.06%	$0.10	
Refunds / Chargebacks	($2.70)	-1.50%	1.50%	1.00%
Merch Proc + CG Platform Fee	($6.13)	-3.41%	3.40%	3.37%
Contribution Margin	$14.89	8.27%		

	Daily	Monthly	Annually		
Volume	250	7,500	90,000		
Revenue	$45,000	$1,350,000	$16,200,000		
Gross Profit	$3,722	$111,672	$1,340,070	8.27%	
Expenses (est)	$500	$15,000	$180,000	1.11%	4.31%
Payroll	$467	$14,000	$168,000		7.14%
Misc		$1,000			3.56%
TBD		$0			-6.39%
EBITDA	$3,222	$96,672	$1,160,070	7.16%	32%

Then, I took a deep breath and made the call.

After the bare minimum of pleasantries, we got down to business. But before I could show off my numbers, Spencer abruptly said, "Okay, Jonathan. Let's talk about your investors. What kind of capital did you get?"

I was immediately derailed. Spencer made getting investors sound so elementary that I felt like a fool for having skipped that step. Quietly kicking myself, I explained to him that I was just "bootstrapping it" right now.

That's what entrepreneurs did in the beginning, right?

Spencer exhaled slowly, and then proceeded to explain to me the vital importance of bringing outside investors on board. Step by excruciating step, he walked me through how it was *supposed* to be done. He described going after investors as a sort of traveling road-show, a carefully staged production designed to rope in big money.

"First thing you do when you get in the room with some of these guys is you pick out someone and emphasize a connection that you have. Like, 'Oh hey, Mr. Williams, I believe you know my dad from the club. I think I've been on your boat.' You break the ice. These are regular folks just like you and me."

"Um—" I began.

He rattled off a series of commands. "Tell 'em the unmet need. Tell 'em how you meet that need. Make eye contact. Go over the top with the visuals. Get 'em excited. Get 'em to think that your idea is gonna be profitable."

"Speaking of profit," I said, "maybe I could share with you some of the num—"

"It's about getting 'em to believe. And believing is about energy. *Tons* of energy. You gotta set that room on fire; give 'em goosebumps."

While Spencer lectured me from his high horse on how things worked, there wasn't an ounce of doubt in his voice. There was, however, plenty of condescension. His tone made it clear that it was a real chore to have to explain the ABCs of the subscription box business to a beginner. He rushed through his advice, and I could practically hear his eyes rolling as he listed out the "rules" of the industry that he couldn't believe I didn't already know.

I tried to ask questions, but Spencer wasn't much of a listener.

Clearly, this was a guy who was used to people hanging on his every word. He dropped advice like he was tossing coins into a beggar's cup. His tone was annoyed at having to spend a moment of his precious time with someone so lowly, but at the same time it was clear that he expected to be adored for deigning to do so.

"Another thing," Spencer said, barely suppressing a sigh. "You have absolutely got to get a woman on board to help with this thing. This business needs a face, and yours ain't it. No one is ever going to buy into this without a woman's input."

I wanted to tell him about the community I had been building and the thousands of followers I had cultivated with nothing but my *own* knowledge of what it was like to be single, but Spencer just kept talking. *Did he really think that you had to be part of a particular market segment to sell to it?* That made no sense, but he sounded so sure, so confident, that I could feel the beads of sweat break out across my forehead.

And he just could *not* get over my lack of venture capital. He returned to it again and again. "You can go it alone if you want to," Spencer said, "but I'll be perfectly honest with you—without investors, you'll *never* scale your company to the size of mine."

There wasn't much more to say after that.

Spencer's certainty that I was approaching the business incorrectly had a profound effect on me. I felt myself shrinking, feeling smaller and smaller as he continued his lesson with a series of self-assured pronouncements. I was defeated.

My company's future—and my own—never felt bleaker.

THE DARKEST HOUR

"How did it—?" My mom saw the look on my face and didn't even finish the question. "Oh."

She invited me in, and we sat at the kitchen table for a moment until I was ready to talk about it. Finally, I shared with her everything that Spencer had told me.

It wasn't just the information he had given me that had upset me. It was also the sense of hopelessness he had left me with when he hung up. I felt disappointed, depressed, and exhausted. The conversation had sucked all the ambition out of me, and I was sure that I would fail. On top of that, I felt belittled. Spencer had treated me like a child, like someone who couldn't grasp the big-boy concepts of investment and finance.

My mom let me get everything off my chest, listening patiently. When I finally ran out of steam, she asked a single question.

"But why?" she asked.

"Why what?"

"I don't get it. Why do you *have* to have investors?"

I shrugged. "Because that's the way it is."

"But was it something specific about your business? Did you tell him what you're doing?"

I remembered the pages of my notebook, filled with facts and figures about SinglesSwag. All of that data, compiled and ready to go; all of those answers to questions that were never asked. I realized that, in his rush to lecture me, Spencer hadn't asked me about the numbers. He didn't know how profitable my venture was. He didn't know how lean it was. He never asked about my expenses, profit margins, shipping costs, or third-party facilities. He didn't even ask that all-important question: what's your acquisition cost per customer?

Spencer didn't know anything about me *or* my business—and he clearly didn't care.

This guy had told me I couldn't scale my business without outside investors, but there was no actual reasoning behind it. It was just blanket advice that he dished out based on narrow ideas and conventional wisdom.

"Maybe he's wrong," my mom said.

"Maybe," I conceded. "But...even if he doesn't know much about SinglesSwag, he *does* know about the box business. So..." I exhaled.

"I just don't think I can do this anymore," I said.

My mom looked me in the eye and said, "You *are* doing it. You're making money, aren't you?"

I *was* making money. I had a little supplemental income, but it wasn't enough to break away from my day job. So there I was, utterly disheartened and saddled with a small-ish business that, according to Spencer, would never go anywhere. It was the entrepreneurial equivalent of a pet goat—it was cute when it was little, but now it was big enough to give me headaches without being attractive enough for someone else to adopt it.

I appreciated my mother's words, but I explained the financial situation to her. Yes, I'd made some money, but it wouldn't be enough to really change my life.

"Maybe not," she said, "but it's more than what you *started* with."

For the first time all day, I smiled.

HUMBLE BEGINNINGS

Here's something about Boca Raton, Florida, that you could probably guess: it's not cheap. So, even though I was making good money at my job in early 2016, I didn't have a whole hell of a lot of money in the bank. In Boca, money tends to go out just as fast as it comes in. If I were a trial lawyer or a plastic surgeon, maybe things would be different, but I was just barely making ends meet.

When I was getting ready to launch SinglesSwag, I had a grand total of $2,000 in my savings account.

Most of that money went to required startup fees. I had to file an LLC and trademark the company name, for starters. Those things weren't optional: I had to have those articles in place to get a tax ID number, and I needed a tax ID number to link a bank account to the e-commerce platform. Fortunately, I knew a young lawyer who cut me a discount on filing all that paperwork.

With a couple hundred dollars left over, I went shopping. I hit Michael's for some boxes, wrapping paper, trinkets, and accessories for a photo shoot.

After that, my savings account was down to $12.63. But that wasn't a huge problem. Everything else I needed was free. I built the website on a free platform. I built the landing page for free. The email service, the Instagram accounts, and all the social media posts: *free*.

When my mom reminded me how my venture had begun, I realized how far I'd come. I also realized that, once in a while, I needed to take my eyes off of the summit and look behind me to see how far I had already climbed. My mom was right: I *was* doing it. I started with $2,000, and I was now bringing in close to five figures a month in profit. It wouldn't buy me a mansion and it wouldn't completely transform my life, but I was a hell of a lot farther down the road than where I started. I vowed to try to stay positive, to not let other people get to me, and to not give up.

Now, whenever I hit a setback or I'm feeling like I should be further along in my career, I think back to those humble beginnings. I remember the bootstrapping of those early days. I also think back to that magical moment when, as I was watching my son play in a flag football game, I got the notification on my phone that I had just received my first order.

Yes! I let out a cheer and raised my hand to high-five the other dads standing nearby. They gave me a funny look, and that's when I realized that the kids were all gathered around the coach for a water break.

It was halftime at a zero-zero soccer match for six-year-olds, and I was cheering like we had just won the World Cup.

So, I looked a little silly, but who cares? I'll never forget that moment. Best of all, I landed that first customer before I'd even started advertising. I earned that order with nothing more than social media hustle. It was only a $40 order (with a coupon), but I felt like spending the whole amount on champagne.

———

That one phone call with a cocky entrepreneur really took the wind out of my sails, and it could have knocked me out of the box business forever if I had let it. That conversation was all the more disheartening because the need for investors was presented to me as a cold, hard *fact*.

Looking back now, I understand that Spencer's opinion *was* a fact to him. It was *his* reality. He had access to the resources that he viewed as indispensable: people who already had money or who had the talent or connections to raise money. Pumping investors was probably a normal part of his world. So, when he started his business, that's exactly what he did—he found someone to put up some money upfront.

What may have seemed like second nature to him was completely foreign to me. I didn't have those resources. I didn't have those connections.

Maybe you are in a similar position. Access to investors might feel foreign to you, too. Most of us, raised in families that live paycheck to paycheck, don't have a foot in the door with the type of people who have thousands of dollars to throw around on angel investing. We don't have wealthy friends or any kind of "in" with the right people.

You might end up having to do what I did: *bootstrapping it.* But guess what? Depending on your business, bootstrapping can actually work. You don't need outside investors to be successful.

While Spencer assured me in no uncertain terms that I couldn't reach his level of success without investors, I eventually grew my business to be twenty times as large as his—and my business is still going. His business, meanwhile, no longer exists. He's likely on the road raising money for his next big idea or tapping into his parent's network of rich friends. Those wealthy, connected types sometimes lack the hunger to see these things through. In a way, that makes sense: if their businesses don't succeed, it's not the end of the world for them. They don't have as much riding on it as you and I do.

Being **hungry is our secret weapon**. It's not a shortcoming,

It's a *superpower*.

When you hear advice, and especially when you hear negativity *disguised* as advice, don't let it get you down. People are usually just telling you what *they* have experienced, and it may not apply to you.

Today, when people come to me for advice, I take the time to get to know their situations. There is no blanket advice that's perfect for everyone. It depends on the type of business, where it is in its lifecycle, and a hundred other factors. If someone asks me for guidance, I make an effort to find out more about their project. I try to remember to ask questions and listen. I promised myself I would never treat anyone the way Spencer treated me, leaving me with an unopened notebook full of questions and a feeling of defeat.

Even if you do receive bad advice, or advice that's not right for your business, remember this: it can still benefit you. After that excruciating phone call, I truly believed that my business was in trouble. I looked into getting investors, but with no luck. Then, believing I had a broken business, I doubled down on the efforts that I was pouring into SinglesSwag. I poured even *more* energy into it, knowing that if I didn't, it would crash and burn.

I did more research, taught myself more skills, and hit marketing even harder.

In the end, that conversation pushed me. It made my healthy obsession even stronger.

Sure, that phone call gave me flashbacks to all the people who had failed to support me in the past, to all the negative influences I've had throughout my life, but I'm actually glad that it went the way that it did. Where would I be if Spencer had loved my idea and offered to invest in it himself? Or if he had helped me to find investors? I would still have the same business, but I would own a lot less of it.

I wouldn't have reaped all the rewards of my own work.

YOU DON'T KNOW ENOUGH

Near the end of our call, Spencer was finally winding down his lecture on the importance of investment, while I waited for a chance to get a word in edgewise.

"So, you just can't go out and start a *real* business without getting proper backing. You'll have to get that in place before you launch."

Finally, I had an opening. "But I already launched."

"Wait…*what?* You launched *without any backing?*"

"Yeah. About six months ago."

I heard sounds through the phone that made me think Spencer was having a minor stroke. But he gathered himself and sputtered out, "That's insane. You're going to need a team. And you can't get a team without money. How are you going to get an operations manager? A customer service manager? A digital marketing manager?" He had a dozen employees at his company, all shuffling around in a bright, clean office in downtown Boca. "What about product sourcing? Hell—how are you gonna advertise?"

"I do advertise. Facebook, Google—"

"But…but…how did you hire someone to manage all that?" He was completely lost.

"Well, *I* manage the advertising."

That's when Spencer laughed out loud. Maybe he didn't believe me. Maybe he thought I was crazy. Whatever the reason, he was getting a kick out of my answers—and not in a good way. If it's possible to hear a smirk through the phone, I heard it that day.

That "get investors" advice is about more than just money. It also assumes that, unless you can bring on people who are more qualified than you are to run the business, your venture won't succeed. Many people look at investor money as "smart money," because it comes with operational expertise. Conventional wisdom suggests that outside experts are needed for success, but that assumption underestimates the power of passion and a willingness to learn.

Your business may, indeed, need an operational manager. It may need an in-house lawyer, a graphic designer, or a team of researchers in a lab. It all *depends on what business you're launching*.

I was selling subscription boxes digitally, so I didn't need a team of NASA scientists to help me figure it out. I found cool gifts, packed, and shipped them, and posted ads on Facebook without a team of expert marketers. It's tedious, but it's *not that complicated*.

Spencer laughed when he found out that I did all my own Facebook ads, but that was actually the key to my success.

When I posted my first Facebook ads, I started off with only $20 a day. By the time I spoke with Spencer, we were spending somewhere around $500 a day (not that he asked), and within a year, we were spending over $10,000 a day—*without* an ad agency or social media expert.

In fact, implementing Facebook ads was one of the primary strategies for scaling my business. I taught myself to do it and I did it well—ultimately better than most agencies could. And I'll be completely transparent—I didn't need to overcome a whole lot to learn how to use Facebook ads. I researched the info on how to set up and run Facebook ads, which isn't rocket science despite what agencies would have you believe. Getting started is time-consuming at first, but it gets easier. The conventional wisdom is that you need an expert. You don't. You just need *time*.

The secret is to really dig in and *master* the use of Facebook ads, and that means immersing yourself in that platform. It's all about testing different versions of ads and using that validation process to continuously refine. I remember playing endlessly with different variants—trying different photos, slideshows, and videos, and then measuring the results. I learned how to do all of those things on my own through the platform and playing with different graphics was free. I didn't need a professional graphic designer. I tested hundreds of different versions of ad copy. I tested ads with coupons and without coupons, and then measured the response. I limited the demographic, I tinkered with my target audience parameters and even learned how we were performing on desktop computers versus mobile news feeds.

Facebook ads were my primary source of website traffic and new customers, and I was growing rapidly, even though I was managing it by myself. And while Spencer assured me that my DIY approach wouldn't be sustainable, it actually *was*. And it was sustainable because I was willing to teach myself the basics, and then dive in and obsess over the tactics.

In e-commerce especially, your marketing funnel is critical. You need to figure out how to convert curious clicks into actual sales. It's more than just Facebook ads—a successful plan also includes Google AdWords, affiliate marketing, email marketing, SMS marketing, and potentially influencers and micro-influencers, among other things. But if you're starting a small business in your garage, don't be intimidated. You *can* learn these platforms, and you *can* master the strategy.

It all comes down to how much you want it.

The great thing about learning all these different skills is that even after you eventually grow, even after you hire someone else to handle those aspects of your business, your knowledge of virtually every aspect of your business will make you a better boss someday. You'll be a more effective supervisor of your marketing team if you know what they're doing. If you threw yourself in and learned it early on, you'll know that side of the business intimately.

If you do attempt to broach digital advertising on your own and you're unsuccessful, there will always be third-party agencies and individuals eager to help. (Trust me, I know. We'll get into that in Chapter 8.) Some of these agencies may even be effective or have a proven track record of success but know this: no one's interest or drive to grow your business will ever match your own.

Successful bootstrapping isn't just about using your own money—it's a state of mind. It's a willingness to hustle, a hunger to learn, and a burning motivation to work hard and learn.

Bootstrapping means staying aggressive; it means not taking *no* for an answer. It means being willing to make more sacrifices than your competition. It means investing your own cash, but also your time, energy, and passion.

BAD PRESS

Bad advice is one thing. At the end of the day, you don't have to take it.

But sometimes, negativity will come at you from a place you never expected. Even after your business is off and running. Even after you have customers. Even after you are profitable.

Even after you thought you had finally put all the haters in their place with a successful launch.

Believe it or not, there will *still* be people who will claim that your business will never succeed.

As I approached the one-year anniversary of my launch, my numbers were looking better and better. By then, I had a team working for me, a third-party facility helping me fulfill orders, and plenty of word of mouth on social media working in my favor. The business was even beginning to garner attention from national media outlets. So, when a woman from the *New York Post* contacted me and requested one of my boxes for a review she was planning, I gladly sent one her way. She sounded nice on the phone, even excited about what SinglesSwag was doing. Getting a mention in a major media outlet could be a big break-through in name recognition and credibility, and I couldn't wait to see what she thought.

A few weeks later, I was blindsided by the headline: "This gift box is an insult to single women everywhere." It became abundantly clear that the writer had planned a hit piece from the very beginning. The sample box I sent included standard gifts: an eye mask, soaps, hand gel, a journal, cookies, and a gold bracelet. These were all items that had proven incredibly popular with our subscribers. Not so much to the reporter, though, who wrote, "to me, they were mostly worthless—and offensive."[1]

Offended? By soap? I didn't know that soap *could* be offensive. I was confused...until I read the article again. There, in the middle of the page, was the line that explained it all. The real reason that the writer was unhappy with my company? "The company founder—not a single lady but a 36-year-old divorced dad named Jonathan Beskin—says they have over 10,000 subscribers."

There was that tired old criticism again, hidden between the lines. *What do you know about single women? You'll never succeed without bringing in a woman partner. You just can't do it.*

But I *was* doing it. I *did* have over 10,000 subscribers. She could have done more homework if she didn't believe me. I had nothing to hide.

This time around, I wasn't going to let a know-nothing naysayer rattle me. My business was acquiring more and more subscribers every month, and I was far more confident in my instincts.

---

1 Doree Lewak, "This Gift Box Is an Insult to Single Women Everywhere," New York Post, March 29, 2017, https://nypost.com/2017/03/29/this-gift-box-is-an-insult-to-single-women-everywhere/.

I *had* been single, I *had* been lonely, and I *had* been in need of a gift. I knew how that felt, and I was certain that there were women who felt the same thing. At this point, it was laughable when people didn't believe it would catch on. If our service was an "insult to women everywhere," how is that we had grown *1,000 percent* over the past four months?

Within a week, the story had been parroted by a couple of other well-known outlets, including NBC News and Mashable, among others. But I didn't let it get me down. I just kept watching our numbers grow. The numbers kept proving me right.

After that so-called bad press, our membership *increased*.

In the end, those hit pieces gave our brand more than just free publicity. They also gave us credibility, because just being on the radar of those national outlets meant something to readers. We were now relevant in the national media, and that notoriety was valuable—whether the *New York Post* reporter liked it or not. We flipped all of those mentions to work in our favor, proclaiming, "as seen in the *New York Post*" and "as seen on *NBC News*" in Facebook ads and on our website.

The takeaway here is that even after you've found some success, **you'll continue to encounter naysayers. Ignore them**—just like you did in the earlier stages of your launch. Not everyone is going to understand your idea, and that's okay. Is it more important that journalists like your idea? Or that your target market likes it? If you ever get bad press like I did, remember that you can make lemons out of lemonade. Use that free publicity to reach more of the people who actually *get* what you're doing and want to buy your product.

GET READY TO WORK

A big misconception in the entrepreneurial world is that you can't survive without investors. People will tell you that you *have* to raise money in order to scale a company and become a real competitor on a national or international level.

It depends on the type of business you're trying to launch, of course, but that formula doesn't apply to every startup. If you don't have a lot of money to start with, focus on an idea that doesn't require significant upfront capital or investors. When you develop a direct-to-consumer (DTC) e-commerce business like I did, you can likely count on not needing much beyond sweat equity to get started.

Conventional wisdom isn't always that wise, and it often prevents people like you and me from taking the first step towards starting a new venture. Don't let it.

I was told that I would *fail* without investors. I was told that I would *fail* without operational help. I was told that I would *fail* without outside expertise. And hearing those things genuinely set me back and made me question what I was doing. I was sometimes devastated to the point of almost giving up.

Fortunately, I never gave up, and that advice was far from accurate.

Plenty of people may have succeeded by following conventional business wisdom, and that's fine. But just because it worked for them doesn't mean that it's necessarily good advice for you. To maintain focus and keep your momentum, you'll need to tune out the bad advice, ignore the naysayers, and use the bad press to your benefit.

When you hear advice that you think is off target, ask yourself whether that advisor really knows you or your idea. Consider whether they really understand your concept and your brand. If an advisor doesn't know you or your business, take their guidance with a grain of salt.

If you're willing to educate yourself and work on a shoestring budget, you can prove some of the naysayers wrong. There are free resources available, and all they cost is *hustle*. It doesn't take a genius to learn how to run a business—that's just what the guys in expensive suits want you to think. You can bootstrap your business as long as you're willing to work harder than you ever have in your life.

If you do decide to take the bootstrapping route, I'm not saying it will be easy. Definitely not! But I am saying it can be done. I know because I did it.

And you can, too.

There will be plenty of challenges ahead. When you set out to build a business single-handedly, you'll find yourself working longer and longer days while sleeping shorter and shorter nights. You'll develop abilities you've always wanted, but you'll also be forced to master at least a dozen different skills that you had no desire to learn. You'll fall and get back up, you'll make mistakes, and you'll have to remind yourself a hundred times why you decided to attempt any of this in the first place.

You'll also feel the rush of triumph and celebrate highs that you've never reached before. And when you do, imagine how amazing it will feel to prove all these naysayers, doubters, and condescending elitist assholes wrong.

So, buckle up. Because at some point along the way, you'll be working in every single role in your company.

KEY TAKEAWAYS

- **Learn** and accept that not everyone who offers you advice has your best interest at heart. There may be people with the best of intentions who just don't commit to understanding your point of view or experiences. Most of the time, they are speaking solely from *their* perspective and offering what *they* would do in a given situation, which may not be the best for *you*. Have confidence in yourself and your abilities, and trust your gut.

- **Reflect** on all the advice and commentary that you receive; take time to process it. That may be as simple as acknowledging that a comment was hateful for the sake of being hateful and moving on, or it may be tearing into a piece of advice you didn't love and seeing what you can glean from it. Give yourself credit in this process. You do have the expertise to be successful and if you do not presently, you have the ability to obtain it.

- **Act** with gusto and trust your instincts. Use any outside negativity or doubt as fuel. When you're doubting yourself or being pessimistic, recognize that it's normal. Pick yourself up, dust yourself off, and look for an opportunity to turn it into something positive. You can do it.

CHAPTER 6

WEARING
ALL HATS

B y early 2016, I'd been in the banking industry for well over a decade. I'd been through many life changes—moving north, becoming a father, moving back to Boca, and getting divorced—but my day job was still in the same field. And it still wasn't fulfilling. So, I finally decided to add a new dimension to my professional life.

I picked up fourteen side hustles.

Sounds impossible, right? No one in their right mind would take on fourteen separate jobs on purpose, but the reality is that this is what starting your own business really looks like. In all the inspirational books for entrepreneurs I had read—and I had read quite a few—no one fully warned me about the sheer volume and variety of tasks that I would need to take on to make it work.

But when you're starting out with just $2,000 and no connections, you don't have a choice: you fill every single role at the company yourself.

I was the Founder and CEO, but I was also the
- Marketing Manager
- Accountant
- Graphic Designer
- Customer Service Agent
- Photographer
- Lead Copywriter
- Sales Representative
- Social Media Coordinator
- Director of Operations
- Research Analyst
- Shipping and Logistics Manager
- Company Driver
- Merchandising Associate
- Intern who fills up the coffee machine and picks up lunch

And if you're wondering, how could you possibly work fourteen side jobs *and* a full-time day job in banking while taking care of a five-year-old son, a dog, and a litany of other responsibilities? The answer is simple:

I didn't. There weren't *enough* hours in the day.

So, I worked all night. I became a nocturnal animal.

On the days that I had my son (he split time between my place and his mother's), my mornings started early. He was still little, so I had to get him out of bed, make his breakfast, and make sure his socks were at least in the same color family. After dropping him off at school, I'd return home and check SinglesSwag's social media accounts. I'd post a few memes or photos, "like" a couple hundred posts, and check the email.

Then I'd tackle my day job. Because it was a remote position, I didn't have all the staff meetings, presentations, watercooler gab, and general time-wasting to deal with. I was typically able to complete all my work—*plus* sneak in a workout and occasionally a short nap—before it was time to pick up my son from school. I'd check the SinglesSwag accounts again, go get my son, drive him to youth sports or other activities, and then bring him home and get him fed. After dinner, I'd bribe him to take a bath and promise him his favorite stories to get him into bed.

Once he was asleep, I'd switch gears. That's when I could finally sit down with my laptop, crack my knuckles, and work on my business from 9:00 p.m. to 3:00 a.m.

That was another full day's work. It just took place while most of the world was sleeping.

This is when all the energy of my healthy obsession kicked in, and I'd spend the hours studying, planning, and executing to continue to grow my company as fast and as profitably as possible. *What more can I do? What's working? How can we do more of that? How can I be even more aggressive? What are our competitors doing? How can we do it better and more effectively?* I turned the problems over and over in my mind to see things from every possible angle. Even the smallest, seemingly insignificant angles were not off-limits. But this time, I was in control of my ruminations. Instead of being driven to distraction, I was making them work for me.

First, I'd put on my Merchandising Associate hat and reach out to new vendors in the constant search for great items to include in the boxes. If I contacted fifty different companies, I'd usually get only a handful to agree to be included, but I didn't care. I kept pushing.

Then I'd switch to my Accountant hat. *Is there a cheaper way to get that done?* I'd put my Merchandising Associate hat back on to find the answer. If I wasn't getting the right price point from one vendor, I'd negotiate hard. If I had no luck, I'd look for a different supplier. Good thing the Accountant and Merchandising Associate worked in the same office—they always had to collaborate.

Someone once asked me if I dreaded those late nights. I thought about it for a moment and realized that, actually, I *didn't*. It was the *day* that I dreaded. It was logging in to that boring day job and taking care of the endless real-world errands and chores that made getting up each morning a total drag. My days were tedious and uninspired.

But the nights? The nights were exciting.

I got to the point where I couldn't wait for 9:00 p.m. to hit. I couldn't wait to put my son to bed, fire up the laptop, and put on my Marketing Manager hat. I looked forward to taking some photos, designing new Facebook ads, and test driving a few taglines for a new campaign. *How can I convince more people to try SinglesSwag? How can I catch their eye?* I would put on my Lead Copywriter hat and brainstorm version after version of headlines and text for the notes included in each subscription box. On a good night, I'd stumble onto a great one, such as: "When you're the love of your own damn life"—a headline that brought in literally thousands of new customers.

I should know; while wearing my Marketing Manager hat, I was tracking all of our leads and where they came from, right down to the particular Facebook ad they clicked on. Facebook provides an enormous amount of data for each ad and understanding the analytics and digital advertising attribution is critical to success in e-commerce.

It was in the nighttime that I found my rhythm. I felt more awake than I had all day. I was aggressive, proactive, and hungry. With each new customer, I got even more excited. I was constantly refreshing the SinglesSwag dashboard, which displayed revenue in real time. It was electrifying to see these numbers climb with every new click of the refresh button.

Some nights, I didn't want to quit at 3:00 a.m., so I kept grinding. At some point in the wee hours, the part of me wearing the HR Manager hat would tell me that I was violating some labor law and that I should let myself go to bed. Even with less sleep, I had never felt better in my life. I truly enjoyed those near-all-nighters. I even bragged about them, when given the chance.

Finally, I had a healthy obsession in my professional life.

A MINDSET SHIFT

For the first time in my life, work wasn't something that I *had* to do. It was something that I *wanted* to do. Maybe I didn't love every one of my fourteen side jobs, but I genuinely enjoyed most of them. I found it deeply satisfying to create, experiment, and strategize. I learned that work didn't have to be a bad thing. It didn't have to be something you suffer through while you prayed for something better to come along.

Those nights confirmed what I had always known: that, for me, having a healthy obsession was a good thing. It gave me a sense of purpose and a place to channel all of my mental energy. The more I became obsessed with SinglesSwag, the more aggressive I got. The more aggressive I got, the more the business took off. The more the business took off, the more I enjoyed it.

At long last, I was on an *upward* spiral. I could feel the trajectory of my life changing, and it felt good.

If you find yourself wearing all the hats at your new startup, don't focus on how much work you have to do—that's the quickest way to get overwhelmed. Instead, **focus on mastering that *obsessive mindset*.** Get into an aggressive frame of mind—the one that is laser-focused on success—and ask yourself what you need to do to make your business better. The more you learn to love the daily struggle, the better you will feel. Bring this mindset with you to every aspect of your work— every hat you wear—so you can improve your business from all angles.

With success as your guiding principle, you'll knock out the to-do list in front of you in record time, because it's no longer a random list of tasks without clear benefits. **It's now a list of opportunities that will get you closer to your goals.** With this mindset, you'll even find that adding *new* tasks to your list isn't a chore. It's something to look forward to because it gets you where you want to go. All those extra hats are now in perfect alignment and working together to build your business.

I should add here that not every task on that to-do list is going to be fun. Starting a business isn't easy, and there will be plenty of fires to put out along the way. But when you've truly mastered the obsessive mindset, every one of those obstacles and challenges becomes a chance to learn and succeed. Even the hard stuff will feed into your healthy obsession as you create a positive feedback loop. Overcoming challenges feels good and gives you even more energy and drive to tackle the next one.

Before you know it, you're on an *upward* spiral. When you get there, **overcoming difficult challenges isn't paralyzing. It's intoxicating.** The harder the problem, the more rewarding it is to overcome. You might even find yourself looking *forward* to big challenges because they're so satisfying to solve.

Embrace your new obsession and get excited to work those extra jobs, whether you have fourteen of them or forty. When you master the obsessive mindset and make it work *for* you, you'll look forward to your mountain of work. You'll see it as a chance to fight for your goals—a chance to change your life.

PLUGGING THE GAPS

You have one unread message.

When SinglesSwag was first gaining steam, I enjoyed connecting directly with customers. Each new subscriber was precious, and I did whatever it took to keep them satisfied and subscribed to the service. I had worked so hard to win the first handful of customers, so to lose even a single one was devastating.

Moments after I received a notification, I'd craft a reply. I knew that customers are inherently impatient, especially in this age of instant gratification. There's an expectation that questions and concerns should be resolved quickly and effectively.

You have two unread messages.

Many of the messages were from potential customers—people on the fence about purchasing SinglesSwag. They asked questions like: *What will be in next month's box? Can I cancel at any time without a fee? Can you include a gift note?* (We can, and frequently do.) I would always prioritize messages from the fence-sitters, hoping to entice them to subscribe. I never lost sight of the connection between customer service and increasing revenue.

You have five unread messages.

A couple of months after launching SinglesSwag, the pace was picking up. It was no longer just a handful of hard-won customers. I now had a couple hundred recurring customers and was juggling a multitude of customer service tasks each day. A lot of these were routine responses, but I didn't trust anyone else to give my SinglesSwag subscribers the white-glove treatment that I wanted them to get. So, I handled each response myself.

While I plugged away at the incoming requests, I thought about that old story of the little Dutch boy who saved his village by plugging a leak in the dike with his finger and holding back the waters all night. That was me: single handedly holding back the flood waters and keeping my business on track. What was the harm? I did this better than anyone, I enjoyed the interactions with SinglesSwag customers, and besides—I was still getting three and half hours of sleep each night.

You have ten unread messages.

I was starting to get notifications throughout the day and during the night. As my customer count crept closer to 500, I still made it a point to reply to each query as quickly as possible. Many of the messages were still routine questions about shipping or products, but for the first time, I began receiving inquiries about the dreaded c-word: cancellation. I had to quickly develop a strategy for customer retention. So even though I was busy with fourteen other jobs, I took on the challenge of creating new and better responses to retain customers. At the same time, I was still fielding questions from those fence-sitters who were considering joining for the first time.

I pictured the little Dutch boy using both hands to plug up more leaks as they popped up. But I was doing okay—I was still getting three hours of sleep a night.

You have thirty unread messages.

By the time 2016 came to a close, our subscription numbers were approaching 1,000, and I started to notice a pattern. There was always a significant spike in customer service emails and messages right around renewal time, and they were often requests to cancel. Typically, I would reply to the flurry of messages with offers to entice them to stay. My mission was to keep my customers excited and engaged, but the sheer volume of requests was beginning to take a toll.

I imagined the little Dutch boy with his shoes off, running out of fingers and toes to plug all the holes in that leaky dike. But I figured I could still handle it—after all, I was still getting two and a half hours of sleep.

You have 100 unread messages.

At that point, I have to admit things were getting crazy. I was checking my email and Instagram all day and half of the night. *Do the boxes have a tracking number? I tried to cancel but my card was charged anyway! Can I order more of the jasmine-infused hand cream from this month's box?* I needed to sneak in customer service time between my banking job, creating Facebook ads, coordinating with the fulfillment center, taking my son to lacrosse practice, and analyzing subscriber demographic trends. Customer service messages were the last thing I handled at night—*I didn't like the politics of that Chelsea Handler book in last month's box!*—and the first thing I handled every morning—*Have you thought about a "teatime" theme for next month's box?*

The little Dutch boy was out of digits. And I was only getting two hours of sleep.

You have way more unread messages than you can handle. Godspeed.

I still needed to go the extra mile to cultivate loyalty and keep customers happy—this was critical to our success. I needed customers to feel good about the brand and get excited about their upcoming box when they saw that monthly charge. It was at this point that I reluctantly began to consider hanging up at least one of my hats. In order to keep my favorite and ultimately most important jobs—CEO, Marketing Manager, and Idea Man—I needed to begin filling some of the other positions with qualified help. I knew that if I wanted to continue to aggressively grow my company and get to the next level, I could no longer do it all by myself.

HANGING UP A HAT

Yes, **you** *can* **do it all when you first start your business.** And in my opinion, what you will learn by wearing every hat is truly invaluable, so maybe you should! You are absolutely capable of doing it all and launching your own venture, no matter what the naysayers have told you—or even what you have told yourself. But if you continue to grow, know this: **you can't do it all** *forever.*

As you grow, it's only natural to need help. Things progress, and little by little, the volume of work will become too great for one person alone. But how will you know when it's time to bring in some help?

Trust me; you'll know.

When your healthy obsession starts to become unhealthy or begins to impede on your ability to achieve your ultimate goals, you'll know it's time to hang up a few of your hats. There's a line between the type of focus that leads to great outcomes and the kind that starts controlling *you*. If you're typing furiously, juggling phone calls, and wishing you had a third arm, you might need some help.

I did the customer service for SinglesSwag all by myself for the first five or six months. But eventually it got to the point that if I continued to try to handle it all, the level of service would suffer. Customers would have to wait for answers to their inquiries—or worse, for resolutions to problems. In the meantime, any delay would increase the odds that they would want to cancel their subscriptions.

And I just could not accept that.

When it's time to bring on employees, don't think of them as just another added expense. If your company is growing, then likely so are your revenues. Hopefully, you'll reach a point where it not only makes sense to strategically free up your time, but you can afford it as well. When you reach that level, it won't *hurt* your profitability at all—in fact, it will *help*. The extra hands will ideally allow the business to run more smoothly while giving you more time to focus on where you're most valuable: aggressive growth. **Approach hiring with the mindset that you are investing in the future of your company.**

I realized that it wasn't admitting defeat to give up some of my tasks. It was a sign of success. Hiring a staff *before* you launch means spending money you haven't yet earned, and it's smart to avoid that when you're bootstrapping, but refusing to hire people after you're making money means potentially limiting your income and growth. By trying to save a few dollars—or worse, insisting on doing everything yourself to the *detriment* of good outcomes—you might actually hold your business back from becoming all it could be.

In my case, before my first year in business was over, I was making more with my entrepreneurial side hustles than I was with my day job. At that point, operating on two hours of sleep just wasn't necessary. For my quality of life, and to keep the company booming, I sat down to assess all of my responsibilities.

I began to prioritize which of my roles were the easiest, the cheapest to fill, and which ones ate up the most time. I analyzed the full list of my duties and decided which ones made the most economic sense to outsource. My goal was to strategically take a little work off of my plate so that I could continue to channel my healthy obsession into areas that would help the business continue to grow.

I also wanted to finally get some sleep.

PICK AND CHOOSE

When your business gets big enough to require employees, you don't have to turn over all of your hats to someone else. When I was going through this process, I remained very cautious and selective about which responsibilities I was willing to entrust to others. I went through my entire list of jobs, assessing each task that was part of a typical week, careful to hold onto the tasks that I knew I could do better than anyone else.

When you're ready to decide which jobs to keep for yourself, it's helpful to consider three categories:

- Jobs you like to do
- Jobs you are good at
- Jobs that are most strongly connected to profitability

Starting with jobs and tasks that you like makes sense, because you got into this business to feel good about yourself and make your life better. If you're anything like me, you'll also tend to get started on these tasks earlier and get them done faster because you're looking forward to them. That means you're working efficiently, so doing the things you like can save you money when compared to hiring someone else.

Keeping the jobs you're already good at on your own plate also makes sense. There's the efficiency factor to consider, as well as the fact that it would take longer to train someone to get to your level of expertise. That training takes time and money, and you can save both by doing the things you're best at.

Finally, there are the jobs that have the biggest impact on your growth and profit. The areas that are most important will vary depending on your business. For example, if you're selling an original product, dealing with manufacturing and shipping will likely have a big impact on your bottom line. For me, keeping new subscribers coming in was critical for growth—and that meant that marketing and customer acquisition-related tasks were more powerful than just about anything else. I happened to love that work, but even if I didn't, I would have kept it on my plate because of its importance to the business.

Once you know what jobs and roles make your list of things to do yourself, it's much easier to pick and choose which tasks you think can be farmed out. Decide which tasks, even if not completed to your *ideal* standards, can be completed *well enough* by someone else to not impact your company's bottom line. Let's be honest—there are plenty of mindless errands and chores in every business. There are follow-ups and check-ins and invoices and inventory that are time-consuming, but they don't have to be completed by the CEO.

Hire for the mundane. Hire for the things with wiggle room for imperfection. Hire for the things you aren't great at and don't have time to learn. When you're clear about what you need, you'll find that your own priorities will become that much sharper and more manageable.

WORKING WITHOUT A NET

By the spring of 2017, SinglesSwag was rockin' and rollin'. Our numbers were still growing, and I had learned that I couldn't wear every single hat. I was ready to hire. We were going places.

And yet, I was still miserably logging into my remote banking job every morning.

I was like that overprotective parent who keeps the training wheels on their child's bike long after the kid is zipping around the neighborhood like a pro. At some point, the training wheels are no longer helpful. They're just slowing the kid down.

In my case, working in the banking industry was my safety net. I still had some lingering paranoia and fear about getting the ax in the corporate world. It had happened to me before, and I didn't grow up with a trust fund or a rich uncle I could ask for help from if things went south. At no time in my life did I feel secure in what I was doing. I *needed* that job.

So, I held tight to all that fear and transferred it to my own business, thinking, *Who knows how long this entrepreneurial luck will last? I better keep my safety net, just in case.* Looking back, I probably played it way too safe—especially considering that after a year in business, SinglesSwag was now paying me *more than* triple what my banking job was. It made no sense to cling to a job that was paying me so much less, but a lifetime of anxiety led me to hold onto a job that I didn't need. I was in the habit of erring on the side of caution—even when it no longer made sense.

In fact, if my boss at the bank hadn't attempted to add more duties to my workload, I probably would've held onto that job for another year. But thankfully, their decision to increase my responsibilities helped me to make up my mind.

I quit.

Now it was just me and SinglesSwag.

It finally hit me: *what was I really giving up here, anyway? Was my day job a safety net, or was it just a security blanket?*

I didn't need the money anymore, so clutching that day job with both hands suddenly didn't make any sense. It wasn't holding me *up*, it was holding me *back*.

Fear can cause us to see our decisions as far more permanent than they actually are. Leaving your day job doesn't mean that you're setting fire to all your old credentials and erasing all your hard-earned skills. If you leave your job gracefully, you haven't burned any bridges. Most companies would be willing to welcome you back in the future if you were one of their better employees—or you could always get a different job in the same industry. With more than a dozen years of banking experience on my resume, I could always have gone back to the industry if SinglesSwag didn't work out. **The *real* safety net isn't the job. It's the skills and experience you bring to it**—and those are never going away. In fact, you're building them up even more with your entrepreneurial experiences.

The key to making the leap from side hustle to full-time job is an honest analysis of how much you actually *need* that day job to get by. Could you still pay your bills without it? Is your side hustle growing? Are you on a trajectory to earn more next year? Answer these questions with logic instead of fear, and you'll make the right decision when the time comes.

It can be stressful to finally take that leap and leave the security of a full-time job. But if you assess your situation and see that your own venture is profitable, stable, and growing—well, there's not as much to lose as you might think. In fact, there's everything to gain, including your personal freedom and the power to achieve the life you've dreamed of. When you remember why you started your business in the first place and you stay clear on those goals, you'll realize that letting go is what you've always wanted.

YOU CAN DO IT...FOR A WHILE

When you're bootstrapping a new business, you're likely going to wear every hat—and that's not a bad thing. What started out as a side hustle may start to feel like fourteen side hustles. This isn't a bug—it's a feature. You'll learn a lot, build your skills, and understand your business from the inside out. All that work will make you the expert on your business, which is exactly as it should be.

If you're still working a day job, you'll soon be juggling an extremely challenging schedule. But you should know...it *can* be done. **Building a successful business means making sacrifices**—giving up movie nights with friends or drinks on the weekends. It will mean giving up some down time, some gym time, and probably some sleep time.

But if you've chosen the right healthy obsession, rearranging your priorities won't feel like a burden. It will feel *right*. You will feel energized, powerful, and whole. Your obsession will be the first thing you think about every day and the last thing you think about every night. **If your healthy obsession is strong enough, you'll make those sacrifices without a second thought.** You'll give up social time to learn about Google Ads. You'll skip your favorite TV show to learn how to get bulk rates on shipping. With a true obsession, you won't even miss those less rewarding diversions.

As your venture grows, it will require more and more time and energy. And that's great. It's confirmation that your idea was as terrific as you thought it was. Celebrate that growth. At the same time, keep an eye on your dwindling time reserves and **be ready to hire help when the time comes.**

If your day job is a remote gig, you'll obviously have more flexibility and freedom to make time for your own business. But even if you work in an office, it's not impossible to get your startup going. There's plenty of dead time during a typical workday, so it's possible to steal a few moments here and there to do research and learn skills for your own business. Read helpful articles during your lunch break, shop for supplies between meetings, and skip the watercooler conversations in favor of building your social media presence. When you're focused on your mission, you'll be amazed at how much downtime you can reclaim.

Eventually, as your business continues to grow, you'll have to make a tough decision about that day job. There will come a time when, instead of helping you with a bit of added security, it's actually holding you back from making money and reaching your goals. If that's the case, you'll have to **summon the courage to let go of your safety net** and embrace the life of a full-time entrepreneur.

Of course, making your business your full-time job doesn't mean you're done working.

You're not even done learning.

Once I made SinglesSwag my only gig, I had to go out and find people to take over all those extra tasks that I could no longer handle on my own. I had to put together a team and trust them with my vision of the company.

But who could I possibly trust with my business, when no one had ever believed in me?

KEY TAKEAWAYS

- **Learn** the ins and outs of your business. When you're bootstrapping a venture, you will likely wear many hats and learn an incredible amount about your business and yourself. The skills you will develop will be invaluable as your business scales.

- **Reflect** on and constantly evaluate what stage you are at with your business. Recognize your limitations. Just because you're capable of burning the candle at both ends doesn't mean you should. Work hard to understand where your time, skills, and energy are most effectively spent and what responsibilities you can and should give up.

- **Act**, don't stagnate. Swim, don't tread water. Don't be afraid to go all-in and bet on yourself. Don't make the same mistake I did and hold onto a safety net when you no longer need it. That day job will be there if and when you need it again, but hopefully you will not.

CHAPTER 7

LEARNING
TO LET GO

S he was back. Acting completely normal.

At first, I hadn't suspected her. Why would I? She came once a week, worked for a couple of hours, and left.

But lately, there had been too many coincidences.

It had started slowly: a stomachache here, an unexplained head-ache there. Maybe she was starting with lower doses to see what I could take. But I was on to her now. I suspected that she had put something in the Oreos. She may have also tainted the Olive Garden leftovers I had the week before. I couldn't be sure. All I knew was that I felt very strangely light-headed after eating both of these items. Now here she was again, and I was worried that this time, she'd ramp up the dose.

I couldn't let on that I knew. I had to catch her in the act. So there I was, in the room adjacent to the kitchen, with the door cracked just a sliver, hoping to get actual proof of what I knew had to be true.

My cleaning lady was trying to murder me.

I know that sounds crazy. But let me explain.

———

Long before I had my own business, before I had a healthy obsession to keep me occupied, all I had was my banking job, my anxiety, and…a series of crazy, threatening voicemails from my dad.

After I reached adulthood, my relationship with my father was still strained. Even after all those years, he still showed very little interest in my life. In fact, he rarely showed that he cared about me at all. At one point, he got remarried and didn't invite me to the wedding. After every interaction with that man, I always felt worse about myself. So, for my own mental wellbeing, I had to finally make the difficult decision to cut him out of my life. I needed a clean break—I simply couldn't communicate with him anymore.

When he realized that I was shutting him out, my dad got angry. He began sending letters and leaving nasty voice messages. In these tirades, he tried to convince me that *I* was the problem, freely rearranging the facts about past events to make himself look better. He swore he would cut me out of his will, and he had always had more financial resources than my mom and I. As his messages grew more and more unhinged, I started to fear for my safety.

Those threatening messages, combined with my natural inclination towards anxiety, triggered profound paranoia. I started to believe that my father was going to try to harm me in some way. At first, I thought he might show up at my house with a gun. Then, when he never came, I imagined he'd try to get to me in a more covert way. Maybe he'd damage the gas line in my house or cut the brakes on my car. My paranoia started to build, and I began to imagine that he might hire an assassin. No hitman showed up, of course. But I wondered if he could have paid off someone close to me.

I had a hard time trusting the people around me. *Were they in on it? Who had he gotten to, and what were they prepared to do?* Maybe it was someone whom I'd never suspect.

Like a cleaning lady.

Anytime I felt even a little bit sick, I suspected my dad was somehow responsible. I would think, *it's starting. He found a way.* Since I lived alone, there was only one person who had access to my pantry. Only one person could be trying to poison me. I started to believe that my dad had paid my cleaning lady to take me out.

Even at the time, I knew it was absurd. I knew that my stomach aches probably meant that I should eat fewer Oreos, and that Olive Garden leftovers should just be thrown out after a few days. But I couldn't suppress those paranoid thoughts.

So, there I was, spying on the cleaning lady through a crack in the door.

She was wiping things down, working her way around the kitchen countertops. When she paused next to a plate of cupcakes, I held my breath. *Oh, shit. It's happening.* But she was blocking my view of the cupcakes. *Is she spiking them with something? Damn it, I can't see…* And then she was past the cupcakes, still wiping.

Shit. I missed it.

I tried to figure out what to do. *Should I go into the kitchen and confront her? What if I'm wrong?*

I considered offering her one of those cupcakes. If she had poisoned them, she'd refuse to try one. *But what if she just doesn't like cupcakes?* If she claimed to be on a diet, I could say something like, "Come on—would it *kill* you to have just one?" Then I'd watch her face to see if she was rattled.

In the end, I didn't say anything. But I did throw out the cupcakes after she left.

I didn't confront the cleaning lady because it also occurred to me that she probably wasn't trying to kill me at all. She seemed like a normal person, living a normal life—like me. Or at least, the normal me who wasn't tortured with memories and messages from my dad.

But, just to be safe, I'd have to keep my eyes open.

Paranoia is a bitch.

TRUST IS NOT OPTIONAL

That period of intense paranoia is well in the past now, and I haven't experienced *that* kind of harmful obsessive thinking in years. Thankfully, my father also no longer harasses or threatens me. In fact, last I heard, he was suffering from dementia. Even if I did contact him, it's likely that he wouldn't recognize who I was, let alone be able to harm me in any way.

But even though that source of anger and turmoil is no longer a part of my life, the effects remain. Like anyone who has experienced emotional abuse, I'll probably be dealing with the fallout for the rest of my life. What that means for me is that it's very, *very* difficult to trust the people around me, since the one person I *should* have been able to trust actively tried to hurt me. My fear of being poisoned is just the most extreme example of my deep inability to trust the people around me for fear that they want to hurt me. I've experienced trust issues for years, and I may continue to experience them for years to come. It has affected my personal relationships, of course, and it also affects my business.

If I had trouble trusting someone to clean my kitchen, how on earth am I going to trust anyone with the business that I've built?

Even when I know that I can't handle all the work myself, even when I *logically* understand that it's no longer possible to wear all of the hats in my business, my gut still tells me *not* to turn over my duties to anyone else.

When I think about delegating work to other people, I feel the old pangs of fear in the pit of my stomach and the anxiety rising through my chest and shoulders. It's hard for me to trust someone to get things done, and sometimes I even feel a twinge of paranoia that they might screw up a project intentionally, just to fuck me over.

Sure, most of these feelings are irrational—and most people don't experience them to the degree that I do. But all entrepreneurs feel at least a twinge of fear when it comes time to delegate. After all, you've likely built your business with your bare hands, bootstrapping the whole thing with your own money and sweat. It's scary to put even a small part of that in someone else's hands, no matter how capable they are.

If you want a serious business, though, it's just not realistic to keep wearing every hat forever. Airbnb may have started with two guys renting out their living room, but it now has over 6,000 employees. As your venture grows, you *will* have to face your fear of delegating.

When it comes to growing a company, trust is not optional.

For some, it's difficult. For me, it was excruciating. So, I started by recruiting the only person in the world whom I was absolutely sure I could trust.

BEST EMPLOYEE EVER

"I don't know the first thing about customer service."

"Mom, you don't have to. You're a smart lady," I said.

"You should call Nathan, remember that boy from temple? Didn't he used to work in customer service? I think it was at Amazon. No, it was—"

"Mom, Nathan is an idiot. And you're smart. I want you."

"Jonathan, I *have* a job."

"And now you have an even *better* one. I'll pay you more than they're paying you."

"No, no. You don't have to pay me anything. Just wait 'til I finish the year, and I'll help you out for free."

"But I need help *now*. This is critical. I'm drowning over here."

"Well, I can't take your money. It wouldn't be right. I'm not going to take all your profits from this thing. You started it. You should reap the rewards."

"Money's not an issue, Mom. I can pay you whatever you want."

Instantly, my mom was curious, because phrases like "money's not an issue" and "pay you whatever you want" were foreign to our family. We'd been eking it out for a long, long time.

"Wait…how much are we talking here?" she asked. "I mean, you don't have to say if you—"

I told her my revenues. She was quiet for a moment.

"Holy shit," she said.

"I know, right?" I could tell that I had her leaning towards the idea, but she wasn't quite sold.

"But I still don't know customer service. I'm a kindergarten teacher."

"Well, do you know how to handle cranky kids?"

"Of course."

"It's very similar."

———

My mother was the only person in the world who I trusted completely.

I knew that my mother would never undermine me. For three and a half decades, she had always had my best interests at heart. Even when others abandoned me or betrayed my trust, I could depend on my mom.

If I was having trouble in school, she would understand. If my career was less than fulfilling, she would listen. If I was going through a rough time, I could depend on her to give me good advice with no ulterior motive. We had a history, so I knew I could turn to her even when I wasn't comfortable handing over SinglesSwag duties to anyone else.

The thought of trusting a stranger with part of my business made me break out in a cold sweat. But when I thought of giving responsibilities to my mom, I wasn't worried at all.

I knew that a long-time kindergarten teacher with no business experience wasn't the best fit for an up-and-coming e-commerce company that had just been featured in a segment on the *Today Show* and in spreads in *Glamour* and *Cosmo*. But I didn't care. The high level of trust that I had with my mom more than made up for her lack of experience. She had been supportive of the business from the beginning and was genuinely interested in seeing me succeed.

There were only two issues that gave me pause. My mom had been a teacher for decades, and I was concerned that if she retired a year or two early, she might give up a percentage of her pension. Also, because my business was still on the rise and hadn't reached its full potential, I was nervous about the future of the company. In the back of my mind, I was always worried that the venture could still fail. And where would that leave my mom?

But that was security blanket talk. The company was growing and bringing in great money, and my mom had been fairly conservative with her savings. She already had a safety net.

I asked her to come aboard.

Thankfully, she agreed.

I'll never forget my mom's first day on the job, when I presented her with a SinglesSwag T-shirt to welcome her to our tiny team of two. It was a good day for everyone.

I still needed to train her, of course, and training took time. I would spend part of the day teaching my mom the system, then go tackle the mountain of customer service messages myself while my mom was still getting comfortable with the job.

It turns out that if you can wrangle a room full of five-year-olds, you can handle anything. Within a couple of weeks, she was catching on. And in less than a month, she was running the hell out of the customer service department. In her case, being a quick learner easily made up for her lack of experience.

My lack of trust led me to hire someone who, on paper, was wholly unqualified to work at my company.

It was one of the best decisions I've ever made.

Today, my mom is still an integral part of the business. She's no longer focused on day-to-day tasks, serving as more of a director of operations now. She's involved in several departments, doing what she does best: supervising and managing our employees, keeping everyone happy, engaged, and productive. She's good at what she does—way better than she thought she'd be.

Bringing my mom onto the team was a good first step in learning to trust others with my business. It was the baby step I needed to start to feel better about delegating some of my responsibilities. It helped me to see that I wasn't the only person in the world who could accomplish these things. Other people could take what I started and keep it running.

Mary and Jonathan in their Fort Lauderdale, Florida warehouse in 2020.

The key to delegating some of your mountain of tasks is to take one baby step towards trusting others. **Start with one employee, someone you know you can trust.** It doesn't have to be a family member—it could be an old friend, a classmate, or someone you've always respected. It could also be an applicant who you clicked with right away. When you're first learning to let go, **prioritize trust over experience or college degrees.** Trust the person you bring on to do their best for you, and then trust that you can bring them up to speed.

Plan for your first hire to take over a part of the business that bogs you down in operational chores. Delegate an aspect of your business that takes you away from focusing on the big picture of growth, profitability, sales, and innovation. No one expects you to trust your first employee with these important areas, but hiring them will give you more time to devote to your high-impact tasks.

For me, customer service was always vitally important, but that job was more about customer retention and less about growing the company in new and exciting ways. Customer service wasn't the component that would take my company from six figures in revenue to seven. I had to be strategic with my time and energy—and bringing on my mom helped me do that.

EMPLOYEE #3

Sometimes you just get lucky.

I had made it over that scary first hurdle—hiring my first employee—by sticking with family. But a couple months later, the customer service requests were still pouring in, keeping pace with the growing number of subscribers. It was too much for either one of us to handle. I couldn't clone myself or my mother, so I faced a scary proposition: how to let go enough to bring on someone else—someone I couldn't be certain had my best interests at heart.

We were buried in messages and emails, though, so I gathered up my courage and put out the word. I went to Facebook again, the same forum where I had received such an underwhelming response to the SinglesSwag launch the year before. Even so, I wanted to start with my own network in hopes of hiring someone I already knew. I put up a post, explaining that I needed help with customer service and waited.

And then I hit the jackpot.

A classmate from my MBA program contacted me. She was working on a PhD at the time but needed a side gig that she could work remotely while she was at home with her kids. She was definitely overqualified for an entry-level position, so I felt very lucky to get her. When you post a customer service job and land someone with a bachelor's degree from Duke and an MBA, you've hit the lotto. But that never would have happened if I hadn't had the courage to ask for help.

When we brought our third employee on board, I didn't even have to show her the ropes. My mom knew the customer service side of the business at this point, so she was able to train our new hire. This time, the training process didn't take me away from the big-picture activities that I needed to focus on. Once your employees are training the other employees, you have started to build an *infrastructure* for your business. **That infrastructure allows your business to start managing itself.**

And that's what you'll need to get to the next level.

As we continued to add new members to our team, I knew that I wouldn't always find people who had earned my lifelong trust—the list is small. So, we put more emphasis on finding people with the right backgrounds and expertise, people who could learn the duties quickly and be able to hit the ground running. It's more important to hire someone who is trainable, eager to learn, and trustworthy than someone with a mile-long resume.

As we kept growing, so did our customer service team. And it's a good thing, too. At our peak in 2020, we were receiving more than 500 emails a day. On renewal days, we would receive over 1,500 unique customer service requests. If I hadn't reached out and brought more employees onto the team, my mom and I would have been wiped out by the workload and not have slept a wink for months. The dam would have burst,

The SinglesSwag team including Jonathan's son Jacob volunteering at a pediatric cancer hospital in Miami (2018).

and SinglesSwag would have been swept away like so many other companies that fail to scale.

LETTING GO

Hiring your first outsider is like leaving your kid at home alone for the first time. Eventually, as a child approaches adolescence, they're fully capable of calling all the right emergency numbers. You have to learn to trust them, as hard as it may be. You have to be able to leave them in charge while you run a quick errand. Sure, it's nerve-racking. Sure, it's uncomfortable. Sure, as you drive home, you expect to see your house engulfed in flames.

But that doesn't happen. Everything usually works out okay (give or take a broken lamp).

Each time you do it, you become more and more comfortable with leaving things in their hands. Soon, you know from experience they won't burn down the house, and you don't worry about it as much.

The same goes for new employees in your growing company. Yes, you will worry about your first employee or two—a *lot*. But if you find people who work hard and give their best, they won't burn it all down. Trust me. For the most part, they want your business to succeed. Maybe they don't have the same amount of ownership that you have, but they have no desire for your business to fail—after all, that would send them right back to the uncertainty of sending out resumes.

When I first turned over my customer service to a team of new hires, I was nervous. I even logged into the email system a few times late at night to review some of the interactions that were taking place. Sure enough, some of the communications were not handled in the way that I would handle them. While the majority of the messages were managed relatively well, there were a few that just didn't reach my high expectations of "do anything to keep a customer."

But what could I do? Criticize my team? Let them know that I was looking over their shoulders? That would hurt morale, and I'd end up losing employees. I couldn't delegate something, and then start obsessively looking over their shoulders to see whether they were doing things right. That's the kind of unhealthy rumination and paranoia I was determined to leave in the past. All I could do was offer helpful suggestions and strategies that the team could use to keep our customers happy.

And then I had to let go.

When you receive over 1,000 messages a day, there's no way you can check every response. As the CEO of a booming business, I had to delegate and move on. I had to trust my own judgment of the people I had hired and trust that everyone was going to do their best.

Your employees aren't going to complete their tasks exactly as you would. And that's okay. But you *can* **create a system and templates that guide them to adhere to your most important principles.**

For SinglesSwag's newly minted customer service department, I created templates for the most common email responses to streamline workflows and standardize the SinglesSwag voice. I also established a specific cadence for our team to follow when dealing with unhappy customers. For example, if a subscriber wanted to cancel, our team was directed to follow a structured procedure:

- **Triage:** Understand and assess the customer's problem, concern, or feedback.

- **Take accountability:** Address the customer's concerns with compassion and understanding.

- **Take action:** Work to proactively resolve the customer's issue by taking a specific course of action designed to turn concerned customers to advocates of the brand. Depending on the situation, this action could include a discount on future orders, replacement products, and, when warranted, a full refund.

The end game was clear: build increased loyalty rather than losing the account. Instead of micromanaging their work, I empowered my team to offer renewal discounts, send replacement items, and do whatever it took to hold onto our biggest asset: our subscribers.

Jonathan and team at a 5k race in Boca Raton, Florida (2019).

It takes time and energy to create these systems and templates, but doing so will give you peace of mind as you step away from these daily tasks. It will make delegating easier to cope with, and ultimately drive better results than haphazardly dealing with issues as they crop up. As your business grows, you can't play whack-a-mole with your problems and expect good results.

These days, I've delegated most of the day-to-day tasks of SinglesSwag to my employees and now serve as a CEO and Chief Marketing Officer. I identified the functions in my business that I truly couldn't give up: acquiring new customers. But even with those roles, I try to stay focused on the big picture—the higher-level strategic thinking. I have a team that gives me support on the administrative tasks like uploading images to ad platforms and pulling various marketing reports. But planning, budgeting, and executing our campaigns is still a critical part of my daily workload.

And I like it that way.

POSITION YOURSELF FOR GROWTH

When it's time to stop wearing all the hats in your growing startup, the first step is to find someone whom you trust.

With your first employee, prioritize trust over experience or background. Find someone you're comfortable with to ease the anxiety of parting with some of your responsibilities.

As you continue building your team, you'll eventually have to hire people you don't know. It's an inevitable part of the growth process. So, when you're considering applicants who haven't yet earned your trust, shift your emphasis to their *experience and willingness to learn.* Find candidates with skillsets that match your needs, those who can hit the ground running.

As you learn to trust new employees with small pieces of your dream, you'll get more comfortable letting go. You'll learn to **back away from the nitty-gritty of everyday operations and focus on the big picture.**

If you attempt to retain control of every task, you'll get less and less sleep and eventually drive yourself into the ground. **Delegating allows you to maintain your obsessive drive without burning out.** Similarly, if you hire a team, but can't let go enough to let them handle the duties in their own way, you'll eventually lose your employees to a boss who doesn't micromanage or rule from a place of paranoia. You'll be in charge of everything once again, but facing an impossible amount of work.

It's important to adopt a more sustainable approach. In order to scale your business, you'll need to shift your focus away from the front lines of execution. You'll slowly steer your attention towards the bigger questions: *Which tasks should be completed in house? Which jobs should be outsourced? Should the team work in person at a physical office? Or will the freedom of remote work inspire more productivity? Are we effectively reaching our target market? How could we shift our strategy to reach new segments?*

Once you hire, delegate, and let go, you can **stop being the one doing everything and become the one figuring out how to do it all** *better*. You'll be free to focus on the most important part of this stage of your venture—growth.

After I delegated away most of my busy work, I was able to focus on scaling my business. I was able to put all of my energy into solving the problems that came with a lightning-fast expansion. I could use all of my time to concentrate on new challenges and find ways to get even more profitable.

But it turns out that I would also spend some of that extra time cleaning up my own bonehead mistakes.

KEY TAKEAWAYS

- **Learn** to let go. Sounds simple enough, right? Letting go is often one of the hardest things a successful entrepreneur must do. Even if you do not have inherent trust issues, turning over aspects of your business (your baby) to someone else is scary. But it's necessary.

- **Reflect** on the most critical needs within your growing venture. What responsibilities are you able to turn over to someone else and what do you need to continue to focus on yourself? What skills or experience does the right candidate need to have? Appreciate how exciting it is to reach a new milestone in your venture.

- **Act** by hiring someone you can trust and have confidence that individual will be successful. After all, they'll be lucky enough to have an amazing trainer— *you!* Since you cannot be everywhere all at once, allow yourself to let go of the responsibility with a larger goal in mind. Your time is likely best spent focused on the big picture, not on everyday operational tasks.

CHAPTER 8

GROWING PAINS

I went over the checklist again. Hundreds of empty boxes, a mountain of decorative wrapping paper, 350 bracelets, 350 bottles of perfume, 350 under-eye rollers, 350 snack packs, 350 journals, 350 scented candles, ten chairs, eight large pizzas, and two cases of beer.

Whew.

By its third month, SinglesSwag had acquired well over 300 subscribers. It had reached the point that I could no longer pack all of the boxes by myself, so I convinced a few friends and family members to come over and help me out. I promised that we would make a fun night of it. "Come on," I urged, "It'll be a party!"

I rearranged my living room and dining room to accommodate a winding assembly line with ten stations. As each box was passed down the line, a volunteer added their designated item to the package. I went through the flow again in my head. *Richard on box assembly, Lauren on tissue paper duty, Ally on books and snack packs. From there, Mel packed the mid-sized items and Mom would oversee jewelry and candles.*

This could actually work.

When evening came, my volunteers trickled in. Ten helpers, willing to work for pizza and beer. Thank God they showed up. I ushered everyone to their stations, cranked up some music, and kicked off the packing party. The boxes wound their way through the dining and living room, filling up as they approached the end of the line, where I did a quality control check before sealing each one. We soon got into a rhythm, and we were knocking it out like pros.

I watched the process with pride. In my first month, I had only forty boxes. In my second month, I graduated to over 100. Now here I was with almost 350. Caught up in the moment, I decided to dream a little. I opened a calculator app and estimated where I'd be in a few months if this rate of growth continued. If I continued to add between 100 and 200 new subscribers every month, by next spring I would have...*over 1,500 subscribers.*

The first month's of boxes from Jonathan's house in 2016 picked up by USPS.

I broke into a smile. Nothing could shake the great mood I was in. I watched my team cranking out the boxes and pictured this becoming a regular tradition. The first Friday night of each month, we'd share some laughs, pack some boxes, and crack open a beer after a good night's work. And it could grow each month. A bigger party would just be even more fun.

I surveyed my living room and dining room, which were packed with people, products, and packaging. I glanced down the hall. If I have to fill 1,500 boxes, how many volunteers would I need? I got out the calculator again. *Oh, wow.* My smile faded. *Fifty.*

I stepped away from my spot in the assembly line to peek into my bedroom. I could fit four or five people in there. I glanced in the guest bedroom—there was maybe room for another three or four. I stopped next to the bathroom in the hall. That means I'd have to fit…thirty-one people in the bathroom.

I was witnessing firsthand the challenges I'd read about in all those business books. I suddenly understood why everyone's first question about a new idea is, "But can it scale?" *Ding!* A notification lit up my phone:

Congrats! You have a new subscriber.

———

August was fast approaching.

With only a few weeks to go, it became clear that I would need to fill over 500 boxes to meet the demand of my growing list of subscribers. It was time to face facts: my beer-and-pizza plan for packing and shipping couldn't keep up with my projected growth. I had to find another option.

Jonathan at SinglesSwag first warehouse in Ohio (2016).

Fortunately, I had made many connections in an online forum for aspiring subscription box entrepreneurs. One recommended a fulfillment center in Fairfield, Ohio, run by a company called

Asperis. I didn't shop around much in my search for a fulfillment partner because I just didn't have the time. Every day brought me closer to my August deadline, and I couldn't throw a packing party that spilled out into my neighbors' yards or onto the street in front of my house.

I had to act now. If I didn't get ahead of my own growth curve, my business would fall apart. Within a week or so, I signed a contract with Asperis and arranged for all of my products and supplies to be sent to their facility in Ohio.

TRY TO KEEP UP

One of the greatest feelings for an entrepreneur is the pride of watching your brainchild take off. When your company shows the first signs of solid growth, you feel almost giddy. It's a lot like watching a child take his first steps. Your fists and forehead are taut with worry, and you're holding your breath, hopeful that today's the day he makes the move. Then, finally, all that tension releases as you watch your baby start to walk. You've never smiled so fully in your life.

With a baby, you probably have time to get it all on film and savor the moment. But with a business, there's no time to celebrate liftoff. As you transition from a do-it-yourself, living-room operation to an industrial-sized enterprise, you'll need to respond very quickly. Critical decisions will come at you with lightning speed, and all you can do is react. Because you're still learning the business, you won't always make perfect choices, which is what makes this stage both thrilling and terrifying.

My regular strategy—obsessing over every detail of my business—would never work at this level. I didn't have time to spend late nights researching my options or reaching out for advice. There just wasn't enough time. I often had to make decisions based on my gut.

When you're wearing every hat and your business begins to grow, you'll be learning at a pace you never thought possible. Your whole life will become a crash course in hiring, manufacturing, negotiating, and logistics. You'll learn everything you can in only a day or two, and then pull the trigger on a major decision. And making decisions while you still feel like a beginner is bound to produce some anxiety.

But the one thing you *can't* do as your business is growing is stand still. You can't freeze in place to avoid making decisions. *You have to act.*

Rapid growth brings rapid change. As long as you stay positive—focusing on the excitement of reaching more customers—you'll survive this stage. You'll make big decisions nearly every day that affect the direction of your company, and most of them will turn out just fine. Some of your decisions will even prove to be highly profitable.

But the truth is that at least a few of your choices will be smack-your-forehead stupid moves. I made plenty of rookie mistakes—I wasted time, lost money, and got bamboozled by some big promises and shiny objects.

And I became a better businessman because of them.

THE FINE PRINT

By the end of 2017, they were all coming out of the woodwork. Dozens of different B2B outfits were courting me. I heard from box manufacturers, marketers, email platforms, customer service outsourcers, and more software companies than you could shake a stick at. They all promised to lower my costs, increase my exposure, or streamline my operations.

I had reached a few thousand subscribers and eclipsed over $5 million in revenue by that point, so I was starting to show up on the radar screens of companies that were in the business of business: ad agencies, shipping facilities, consultants. They all started reaching out to me in hopes of getting their own little share of my newfound success.

Some of these suitors were third-party fulfillment centers, and some of them were offering me pretty sweet deals. Unfortunately, my products and supplies were still parked in Fairview, Ohio, with Asperis. And now that I was seeing these enticing offers from other companies, my existing deal with Asperis wasn't looking all that great. Not that I was in a hurry to jump ship—I knew that it would be a hassle to cut loose and relocate my operations to a new facility. So I contacted Asperis to see if they would match some of the deals that I was being offered. I figured it would be a win-win—they'd keep my business, and I wouldn't have to move everything to a different city.

I was sure that Asperis could beat the deal they had offered me at the beginning, when I only had 500 subscribers. We were now dealing with over five times that volume, and I knew that as the volume grew, their profit per box grew as well. Just as it's cheaper to buy in bulk at Costco, it's also cheaper for companies to deal in bulk than it is to hire people and fire up operations for a small project. I knew Asperis was making more and more money as SinglesSwag grew, while my cost per unit stayed exactly the same.

So, I asked them for a better deal. I felt totally confident as I used one offer to negotiate another. I felt like I was getting the hang of the game. So, I was caught off guard by their counteroffer—lots of legalese, but the translation went something along the lines of, "You'll stick with the contract and like it."

Pallets of SinglesSwag boxes at Ohio warehouse (2017).

Wait...what was in that original contract? I searched my computer, found a PDF copy of the agreement, and started reading it more closely.

It was a *three-year* contract.

I was only halfway through. I was locked in at beginner prices even though I was becoming one of their big players—and still growing. The contract didn't have a pricing structure that was flexible or became more favorable with scale. I would pay the same price per unit for them to pack and ship 500 boxes as I would for them to pack and ship 20,000 boxes. They were going to make a fortune off of me.

Although it was a three-year contract, there was no minimum spending requirement I had to hit, so I attempted to leave. Asperis immediately got their attorney involved and refused to release my inventory without a fight. The only way I could get out of my contract would be to send a lawyer up to The-Middle-of-Nowhere, Ohio, and sue my way out of it. It wasn't the best situation, and I was in no position to negotiate. It was my signature on the contract, and I couldn't claim they had cheated me or reneged on their terms. It was all right there in black and white.

SinglesSwag was growing explosively, so I had more important things on my mind than interviewing lawyers to send up north. In the end, I worked out the best deal I could with Asperis—with absolutely no leverage—and decided to grin and bear it for the remainder of the contract.

———

In my haste to move my operation out of my living room, I naïvely jumped into a contract that didn't allow for growth. I rushed the decision, and in the process made two big mistakes.

First, it was a mistake to sign a contract that didn't scale my unit price lower as volume scaled up. This error cost me some money, but I learned a lot from it. I learned what to look for when hiring third-party resources—namely, flexibility, freedom, and sliding schedules that adjust with growth. Today I know the importance of these clauses, and I'm in a much stronger position to ask for what I need and negotiate to get it. I also now know that I can walk away if an offer isn't working—there will *always* be another offer from someone more desperate to work with you.

Second—and it's not easy to admit this—it was a mistake to sign a contract without understanding its full implications. As much as I would like to say that Asperis cheated me or preyed on my lack of experience, that's just not true. At the end of the day, *I* was the one who signed without fully appreciating what that three-year lock-in would mean for SinglesSwag. I made the decision to skip over the fine print, and it cost me. Taking ownership of that mistake is the only way to learn from it.

As you scale your business, there will be times when you just plain screw up. You'll make mistakes, and some of them will cost you serious money. But you can't let that stop you. You have to keep moving forward, making decisions, and doing the best you can with the information that's in front of you.

Your world will be changing rapidly, and there's no way that you can make the perfect call on every single business decision. You'll miss a few details here and there, but usually those unforced errors won't be enough to stop or even slow the momentum of your growth. If you continue to focus on growth, with each contract, you'll get a better deal.

In the meantime, try to forgive your mistakes. After all, you're operating in a shifting landscape, and what was a sweet deal one month may start to look like a rip-off six months later. Take what you've learned and use it in the next negotiation. You might have lost a bit of cash, but you can make it back on the next couple of contracts. You'll get better and better at the game, so be patient.

SinglesSwag grew at a much faster rate than I anticipated, which led to mistakes. But I tried to never make the same mistake twice. After my fulfillment center contract ended, I was aggressively recruited by several other companies. One particular company in South Florida, Shipmonk, was hungry to get my business and they offered me much more favorable pricing than our previous partner. We signed the deal, and our new partner paid to move fifteen truckloads of product—a couple million units of inventory—down to their facility in Florida. And the best part of the deal was that, if we ever became dissatisfied with their performance, we had the option to dissolve the partnership with just *thirty days' notice.*

And I know that little detail because this time I read the fine print.

SHINY OBJECTS

It was 2018, and SinglesSwag revenue was closing in on $10 million, *annually*. I'd built a damn lucrative business, one Facebook ad at a time.

But somewhere in the back of my mind, I still believed that there were people out there who knew more than I did about the ad game. So, when a big-name marketing firm showed me their pitch, I was easily reeled in. Then, when I saw their list of clients—names like Procter & Gamble, Nutrisystem, BirchBox, and HelloFresh—I was even more impressed. *If these big brands were using this agency, why shouldn't I? Who was I to think that I knew better than those guys?*

I hate to admit it, but it was probably the slick presentation that hooked me. That and the New York City address.

The agency proposed a strategy that's increasingly common these days: they slip your brand name into online content that doesn't feel like advertising. They write up articles that appear to be impartial, which they drop into the social media feeds of your target audience. Clicking on these posts directs consumers to publications that are either *owned by the ad agency* or *paid by the agency* to publish the content.

For SinglesSwag, they would generate lifestyle articles mimicking the style of articles in *Cosmopolitan* and other well-known women's lifestyle publications to resonate with women. Articles with titles like, "Eleven Ways to Live Your Best Life in the Summer of 2019." Then, at number three on the list, they'd sneak in an entry with our product: "Love yourself with SinglesSwag."

The agency promised to track the effectiveness of those camouflaged ads using an avalanche of data that they would collect.

I opened up my wallet.

Their service was not cheap. They wanted us to kick off the campaign with a spend of $50,000 a month. They urged us to go big right away so that they could gather the data they needed. And I did go big. Over the next year and a half, I shelled out over *a million bucks* for this hotshot New York agency to grow my company.

And we did grow...*some*.

The agency had a whole team that constantly engaged with us. They'd hold weekly calls and give us a mini-presentation on their efforts—always providing data to prove how effective their campaign was.

The agency team was very slick in how they spun the data. When they placed one of their articles, they would claim every new subscriber within several days of the article's appearance. But here's the thing—we were *already* growing before I met these guys. And even after hiring them, we never stopped placing our regular Facebook ads. So we weren't sure how many new subscribers could be attributed to the work of the agency and how many could be attributed to our own ads.

After shelling out big bucks for well over a year, I decided to take a closer look at what this massive expense was really getting us. I dug into the numbers.

It wasn't that they were scamming us. Not at all. It's just that they were claiming every new subscriber when it wasn't at all clear that they had actually acquired those new customers for us. It wasn't as cut and dry or as scientific as they had presented it. After comparing their data to our own, I concluded that there was a fair amount of *duplication*, with both of us hitting the exact same customers with our efforts.

I hired that firm to help us scale up more dramatically, but the bottom line is that we probably could have gotten similar results on our own. And I could have kept all or most of that million-dollar spend for myself.

———

As you build on your success and people start to see you and your business in the media, get ready.

They're going to try to sell you stuff.

When your business hits a certain size, everyone will want a piece of the pie. Every agency and consultant in America (and often many outside of America) will come after you, and they'll sell you hard. You'll dismiss many of them, seeing right away that they're either total amateurs or just not a good fit for your company. But there will be other suitors—slick, polished companies that have worked with all the brands that you dream of becoming.

You'll see Madison-Avenue pitch decks that will knock you out. They'll make you feel like the center of the universe and promise to tailor a strategy just for you. They'll offer to throw their entire company behind your mission. In fact, they'll promise you the moon and stars in terms of results—if only you're bold enough to bring them in.

It's hard to resist that kind of wooing.

Some of these companies really *may* be able to help you, but it's important to figure out what you need and what you don't.

Now is the time to take everything you've learned in these first couple of years and apply those lessons to these big decisions. You're not a rookie anymore, so you should look at the details, read the fine print, and trust your gut. If your marketing strategy already has your company exploding, don't be too quick to tear it apart and change course. And when it comes to those big-city advertising wizards, don't automatically assume that they have some magic touch that you don't.

Instead of grabbing at the shiny object that's dangled in front of you, step back and assess what your company truly needs. You don't have to say yes to any of the people courting your business. Once you have identified your company's weaknesses, *you* can reach out to a partner that you think would help you grow.

If you do bring in a high-priced outside firm—or even a low-priced one—be sure to track the results yourself. There are hundreds of different ways to spin data to make the numbers look better than they really are. *Keep your own scorecard* to decide whether or not your investment is paying off, rather than blindly trusting the data you're being fed. By tracking results on your own, you'll be able to tell if third parties are delivering what they promised—and if they're worth what you're paying them.

In the future, I'll never agree to an arrangement that requires a huge ad expenditure right from the beginning. Instead, I'll opt for a slower, more intentional process—testing smaller ad runs, and then assessing the impact they have. If the results look good, I'll cautiously raise the spending amount and approve more ads. That strategy worked with our Facebook ads, and it can work with other types of advertising and acquisition strategies as well.

As you continue to scale your business, you'll most certainly catch the eye of some pretty slick agencies and consultants with smooth-talking sales professionals. They'll do their best to woo you and take a cut of your growing profits. You can listen to the pitches, but don't get lured away from the strategies that helped you grow in the first place. And if you do decide to grab one of those shiny objects, make sure that it actually helps your bottom line.

Never lose sight of the fact that it was *your* leadership and strategy that got your venture to this level.

PRIVATE LABELS

When SinglesSwag first began, I was only ordering a few hundred units of each product to fill the boxes. I was dealing with indie producers—many based in the US—that manufactured small amounts of product, some even by hand. That strategy was fine for a while, but the cost per item was fairly steep—and this substantially lowered my profit margin.

So, as I grew, I negotiated better deals. When I ordered 2,000 units, I could bargain for a better price than when I ordered 350. And when I ordered 10,000 units, I could get even *more attractive* pricing. I negotiated hard, and that led to an increasingly higher margin on each box we sold. I negotiated until I was blue in the face. But after the subscription numbers grew past a couple thousand, some of these small domestic manufacturers simply couldn't supply the quantity of product I needed at the low cost I was looking for.

I started looking at the bigger, more recognizable brands. I was cutting deals with well-known brands featured in stores like Ulta, Sephora, and Nordstrom, and they worked with me on price as we grew. Most of the brands we worked with produced their items overseas, often at their own facilities, and were large enough to offer attractive deals when I was ordering tens of thousands of units. As each order increased in size, we were offered better terms and pricing. Once our orders ballooned to 30,000 units, some of these established brands offered to produce new items specifically to meet our needs.

But you can only negotiate so far, and the price efficiencies with established brands that we had achieved with scale were approaching their limit.

I pushed the manufacturers as low as they could go on price. When I hit 50,000 subscribers and was pressing my producers harder and harder for deals, some of them started to balk. In fact, some of the brands got offended by my lowball offers and wanted to walk away. I had lowered my costs again and again and again, but now I was hitting a cement floor.

But I was obsessed. There had to be a way to keep increasing profits.

Just as I did in the early days, I decided to study my competition. Specifically, I looked at the box companies with the most subscribers. I took particular interest in the leading women's subscription box—a well-known outfit with over a million customers. Maybe they knew a few secrets that I hadn't unlocked yet. I checked out their products.

Many of my competitor's brands were well known skincare products from Murad and Kate Somerville, beauty products from Fenty, and fashion offerings from Kate Spade and Michael Kors. It was an impressive lineup. I had even gone after a few of those producers myself. But there were also a few products that caught my eye for a different reason.

There were brands that I didn't recognize.

When I was just an ordinary single dad, there were plenty of beauty brands I didn't know. I thought MAC was a computer and Bobbi Brown was a singer from the '80s. But after immersing myself in the world of women's brands for four solid years, I thought I knew every label out there. *How could I have missed these?* I was surprised to stumble across completely unknown brands. So, I had to know more. And after a bit of digging, I made a discovery:

These subscription box companies were creating their own brands.

It made perfect sense. The in-house brands and product lines looked and felt just as high-end as the established brands, but they saved them a bundle. The big beauty and fashion brands can only go so low on price because they still need to cover their own costs—all those offices, salaries, and marketing campaigns aren't cheap. The best way to get around Clinique's markup is to *become* Clinique. The only way to go lower than Kendra Scott's lowest price on designer jewelry is to manufacture your *own* jewelry. Cutting out the middleman by making your own products is key to increasing profits.

I had already pivoted from small domestic producers to big, multinational brands. Now I was going to pivot again and get into the brand business. And I knew exactly where to start— with the product that was in every single box we'd ever put together.

It was time to make our own jewelry.

At the paper manufacturer in Miami with the first redesigned
SinglesSwag box off the production line (2020).

Suddenly, I had a new healthy obsession: manufacturing. I immersed myself in every aspect of production, from raw materials to pricing to quality control. I quickly learned that I had been buying jewelry from middlemen at a *100 percent markup*, so I knew that I could save my company a lot of money by starting my own brand. I dove right in.

I won't tell you that launching your own brand is easy. It's not. In the beginning, I stumbled a few times. I even lost money trying to negotiate directly with Chinese production facilities myself, not realizing that a single paperwork error could lead to exorbitant importing and exporting duties that inflated the final price. But I didn't give up: I did the research, found a domestic company to handle foreign transactions for me, and bounced back. Instead of trying to oversee every detail of production, I delegated that responsibility and focused on what I'm good at: product design and positioning.

In the subscription box business, perceived value is everything. If the consumer receives a $200 necklace in a clear plastic sandwich bag with no labeling versus a $5 necklace in a beautiful, branded box, they'll prefer the latter every time. So, I focused on creating quality products in packaging that reflects that quality. Consumers want items that *look and feel* like the brands they love, so that's what we aimed to deliver.

Moving into manufacturing and cutting out the middleman ultimately saved SinglesSwag a fortune and made the business more profitable. And even more importantly, introducing our own brands didn't impact the consumer experience. After our own jewelry brand proved to be a hit with our subscribers, we invested in that strategy even more.

February 2023 SinglesSwag Box marketing image

SinglesSwag now owns seven different jewelry brands, some of which have their own e-commerce sites. We've also developed over twenty unique brands in the skincare, cosmetics, and lifestyle sectors. We produce everything from face cream to vegan leather cosmetics bags. These days, when you receive a box from SinglesSwag, around 70 percent of the products will be from brands that we've created in-house specifically for our customers.

———

When I started SinglesSwag, I didn't know anything about developing brands, product design, or manufacturing. But as my business scaled, learning more about and implementing these strategies saved my company a bundle and increased my individual skill set significantly. Not only did it help my venture stay profitable, but it also established opportunities for success in the future. We've now laid the groundwork for several potential income streams. For example, if the subscription box business fades in popularity, we can market our own in-house brands directly to the consumer and give these products a life of their own.

As your own venture grows, keep your eyes open for opportunities. If you ever hit a plateau—as I did when trying to lower my costs—there is usually a creative way to push beyond that and take your business to the next level. Don't be complacent when you see growth, profits, or customer satisfaction leveling off. Keep an open mind, keep learning, and keep looking for new directions to explore.

Your healthy obsession will take you to places you never imagined.

TURN MISTAKES INTO OPPORTUNITIES

As an entrepreneur, I made plenty of mistakes. And you will, too.

There's no time to sit around and dwell on the times you screwed up or lost money. There are too many other things to obsess about—things that can actually help you grow your business. If you do sometimes get stuck ruminating about a misstep, it's important to put a positive spin on it.

Focus on the lessons you learned.

Looking back on my experience with that third-party fulfillment center in Ohio, I'm genuinely *glad* that it happened. It taught me to read the fine print and pay attention to details. And when I remember burning through a million bucks with that New York marketing firm, I'm not angry. If I hadn't spent all that money, I would never have learned to ask tough questions of "experts" and strive to understand the finer points of marketing. I would never have learned to get a second set of eyes on a big contract before sealing the deal. And I wouldn't have the same level of confidence and expertise that I do today.

Instead of stewing about your mistakes, use the lessons to help your company evolve. When you lose money on a deal, chalk it up as the cost of your business education. As long as you don't repeat the same mistake, you'll capitalize on your learning on your way to even greater success.

The growing pains that come with scaling a business are inevitable, but they don't have to slow you down. If you keep your eyes open for opportunities, you'll find many new ways to build profit and emerge as a stronger founder and leader. Don't be afraid to branch out and explore other areas as your business grows—even if you'd never given them much thought before. Controlling more of your own processes and products can help you grow *and* diversify your revenue streams.

After three and a half years of learning from many mistakes, I was continuing to improve and making better decisions. I was negotiating more favorable contracts, improving how I dealt with outside vendors, and manufacturing millions of products a year within our new suite of brands to increase profit margins. I had come a long way.

I was finally gaining confidence as an entrepreneur, and I was sure that I could handle anything that came my way. For the first time since I started this venture, I felt genuinely optimistic. I knew that with everything I'd learned, the coming year would be way less stressful than previous years. *Next year should be a piece of cake*, I thought. *I can finally relax and reap the rewards of what I had sown.*

I was ready to turn the calendar page and just enjoy the upcoming year: 2020.

KEY TAKEAWAYS

- **Learn** to always read the fine print. Rapid growth brings rapid change and it's critical to stay focused on the details. If you decide to grab one of those shiny objects, make sure it positively impacts your bottom line. Never lose sight of the fact that it was *your* leadership and strategy that got your venture to this level.

- **Reflect** on the mistakes you will inevitably make and the learnings they will inevitably yield. Lean into growing pains. Pizza and beer may get you over a hump, but if you are going to scale, you can't remain comfortable. Accept that you will be dealing with varying levels of discomfort until the day you close or sell your business.

- **Act** by turning mistakes and failures into opportunities and wins. The growing pains that come with scaling a business are inevitable, but they don't have to slow you down. As long as you don't repeat the same mistake, you'll capitalize on the learning on your way to even greater success.

CHAPTER 9

FINDING STRENGTH THROUGH THE STORM

I listened to the voicemail again. "Jonathan. We've got a problem. Call me."

It was Scott, the intermediary who coordinated all the Chinese manufacturing for SinglesSwag. I rubbed the sleep out of my eyes and checked when he had left the message: Wednesday, January 22, 7:01 a.m.

Why did he call so early? He knows I'm not a morning person. I stumbled to my bathroom, splashed water on my face, and started towards the kitchen to put some coffee on. But then I hesitated. *He knows I'm not a morning person.*

Even after I delegated many of the menial tasks of my business, I still kept a night owl's routine. I was usually more productive late at night, long after the chaos of the day had settled down. Everyone who worked with me knew my hours, yet Scott had called just before sunrise. Something wasn't right.

With a sense of dread, I grabbed my phone and called him back.

"We have an issue at our production facilities," he said.

My mind raced. I thought of all the things that could go wrong at a factory: equipment failures, logistics glitches, worker protests—*do they even have those in China?*

"You've heard about the virus over there, right?" he said.

I'd seen a few clips on the news. Some new virus had hit a city in China. But the reports made it sound like it was contained, and it seemed a million miles away from Boca Raton. It also seemed like just another sensationalist story. Over the years, I had heard panicky reports of epidemics that never lived up to the fears: SARS, swine flu, Ebola, and the Zika virus. A "pandemic" seemed like something that news websites splashed in their headlines to get clicks.

"I thought that was just in Wu-something," I said.

"Wuhan. It *was*," he said.

"I thought it was contained."

"It's not."

"It's *not* contained? They're not going to shut us down, are they?" I asked.

"Hopefully not. It depends on the case counts."

I was in disbelief. China's lifeblood is manufacturing. "I mean, there's no way they're going to shut down factories. They can't."

"In Hubei province…they're talking about shutting down *every-thing*," he said. "We need to prepare ourselves for possible prod-uct delays."

At the mention of *delays*, my heart started pounding. *Oh, shit. Our next shipment has to go out soon.* I tried to slow my breathing, but I've never been great at that. "Scott, could you hold on a second?"

I needed some air. I flung open the back door, but instead of the sweet, balmy Florida air I was expecting, a blast of cold hit me. I had completely forgotten that Boca was hitting record low temperatures that week. Standing there in my gym shorts and T-shirt—with an icy breeze hitting me—did *not* calm my anxiety. I slid the door shut.

"Jonathan? Are you still there?"

"Yeah. Sorry," I said. "How long would a shutdown last?"

"Nobody knows."

"Is there a cure?"

"No."

"Is it coming here?" I asked.

"Nobody knows," he said.

"But what are you hearing?"

"Are you sitting down?" he said.

I sat down.

"From what I'm hearing..." He exhaled slowly, trying to steady himself. "It's gonna be *everywhere*."

I was quiet for a moment, letting that sink in. I should have known that something bad was coming. When the weather services warn of a cold front so severe that you should watch for iguanas falling from trees, it's probably a bad omen. What plague was next?

"So, what do I do?" I asked.

"Do you know what an N95 mask is?"

———

In your entrepreneurial journey, there will be difficult circumstances that you just can't predict, and no amount of preparation can get you ready for these challenges.

The COVID-19 pandemic was definitely one of those unforeseen challenges. It felt like the whole world was blindsided. From late January through February of 2020, my anxiety levels rose with every news story about the coronavirus. The situation was surreal. Now that SinglesSwag's goods were produced via Chinese manufacturing, the crisis was threatening my livelihood and the livelihoods of every single person that I employed. This was well before the virus affected everyday life for most Americans, though. So, while I bit my nails and lost sleep, other Floridians worked on their tans or played pickleball (of course). Snowbirds from the Northeast filled the shops and restaurants all over Boca, and no one seemed to have a care in the world. Except me.

But by early March, numbers in the US were rising. It was becoming clear that we were headed for a true epidemic right here in our own country. As the case counts grew and we barreled towards the unknown, I had to face a very uncomfortable truth: *nothing was in my control.*

I had no control over whether the factories in China would stay open, whether trans-Pacific shipping would continue, or whether my fulfillment center in South Florida would shut down. I had no influence over the US Postal Service, UPS, or FedEx. I was nothing more than a spectator, watching the drama unfold on TV as federal, state, and local officials responded— often in confusing and contradictory ways.

Worst of all, I couldn't control how consumers would react.

Would everyone lose their jobs? Were we headed for another Great Depression with bread lines and a spike in unemployment? Would people cut out the extras first, or would they want and need a little joy in their lives? Would they be willing to wait months for packages if shipping slowed? What if postal workers quit in droves because it wasn't safe to touch people's doorknobs and mailboxes anymore?

I could spend hours ruminating on all the possibilities—and I often did. There were just so many unknowns. And unknowns meant that I had no control over what was next.

If I couldn't control consumer reaction, I couldn't control sales. If I couldn't control sales, I couldn't control revenues. With no control over revenues, my business would start to spiral downward. And if I didn't have this business, I'd have to go back to banking. *More like back to prison,* I thought. *I could lose everything: my job, my home, my whole life.*

I knew I had to avoid these mental tailspins. I had to keep from ruminating on the negative possibilities.

By the middle of March, the world had ground to a halt, and I couldn't do a damn thing about it.

Because of my obsessive nature, I had controlled every part of my venture for a long time. I had taught myself every skill, I had negotiated every deal, and I had worn every hat until I was forced to delegate. But now I faced a situation that was completely out of my hands. I was a control freak forced to sit in the passenger seat during the biggest economic and societal disruption in generations.

It sucked.

I felt totally powerless. I didn't think that the business I had built was going to survive. Virtual businesses like streaming services or YouTube would be fine, but SinglesSwag was a *physical* gift delivery business. We had boxes put together in person, delivered in person, and given to people who were now literally cowering inside their homes. I didn't think the facility that built and shipped our boxes would stay open. I didn't think that delivery services would be able to get our boxes to people's homes. And, with everyone spraying and disinfecting everything, I wasn't sure that customers would even want to receive unnecessary packages. *What if they were a Trojan horse that brought an incurable disease to their doorstep?*

When the lockdowns were announced, I was panicking. It looked like we wouldn't even be able to get the product we had ordered—and paid for—into our Florida facility. That was tens of thousands of dollars down the drain, and there would be no getting it back when customers started to cancel in droves. If they were now out of work, a subscription box would be the first luxury to go. Much of this time period is a blur, but I remember calling my mother and saying, "I think this whole thing is really over."

I was sure that I was staring at the end of my entrepreneurial dream.

I was powerless to change the course of the pandemic, but I did try to find healthy obsessions to keep me from ruminating on the negatives. In those early days, I was on the phone constantly. I was calling our facilities daily to make sure they were operational, checking in with our China contacts. I was monitoring the case numbers in every state and in more than a few countries, noting where the outbreaks were growing faster and where they were leveling off. I was reading articles, watching for possible reopenings, and trying to predict whether the disease surges in the US would mirror what had already happened in China and Europe.

But there was one possibility that I didn't research, and one that I couldn't see coming. And it changed my life forever.

NO F'ING WAY

By the beginning of April 2020, all of Scott's wintertime predictions had come true. Coronavirus had *not* been contained, it *had* spread everywhere, and I *did* need a good mask. We were now two weeks into lockdowns, and I had landed right back on the same couch where SinglesSwag was born.

Like the rest of America, I needed a haircut, I hadn't shaved in two weeks, and my clothes were wrinkled. It was kind of an entrepreneur-meets-prison-escapee look. I turned off the video option on Zoom meetings and went audio only. I was surviving on frozen meals and food deliveries. I'm sure my sodium levels were off the charts.

I was missing routine interactions with coworkers at the SinglesSwag office. I could suddenly relate to Tom Hanks' character in *Cast Away*. I could have had entire conversations with houseplants if I had any. It was just me, my sofa, and pages of digital data for my company. Without the distraction of trying to keep my business afloat, I probably would've started talking to volleyballs, too.

I had been obsessively checking with my fulfillment center, my shipping partners, and my Chinese connections. But now that the US was mostly closed, I could do nothing but sit on that sofa and plan a funeral for SinglesSwag.

Our subscriber numbers had held steady for the first couple of weeks, but when it was announced that the lockdowns would be extended, I braced for mass cancellations. I assumed that shipping would become impossible and my fulfillment center would close. Most of all, I figured that women just wouldn't be interested in jewelry and face creams when they couldn't even leave their homes.

Our policy stated that subscribers had to cancel by the fifteenth of the month in order to avoid being charged for the next month's box. So, I was watching the numbers like a hawk on the weekend of April 11 and 12. So far, the subscription stats were holding steady. We even gained a few new customers.

But I had a bad feeling about April 15.

That morning, I was more than a little anxious. I glanced out the window, checking for plagues of frogs, locusts, or falling iguanas—with the litany of bad news on TV still going strong, who knew what would come next? As I fired up my computer and logged into the system, I was already brainstorming a plan to steer the ship through the coming storm.

I could lay off half of the customer service team. I'd let them know that they're eligible for unemployment and that I would even help them file the paperwork if they weren't sure how to start. I would keep a core team—maybe a manager and two reps. Based on the latest numbers, I could put a freeze on all new products until I knew how bad it would be, and then we could start working our way through old surplus inventory.

My mind was racing with these possibilities when I sat down to look at the April 15 numbers.

There was no spike in cancellations—in fact, our membership numbers had jumped. A lot. I couldn't believe what I was seeing. I was suspicious that it was some kind of mistake, so for the rest of that week, I was glued to the subscriber numbers, watching to see if the fifteenth was just a blip on the radar or if this was something more.

Slowly, over the next couple of weeks, the truth came into focus.

This was real.

Before COVID-19, we were cruising along with just over 200 new customers a day. But a few weeks into the lockdown, we saw these numbers swell. In fact, they doubled. And then…they increased even more. We watched in amazement as our numbers went up to *over 700 new subscribers a day.*

With every restaurant and bar in America temporarily closed, single women from San Diego to Saratoga Springs were trapped at home, and they needed a gift to raise their spirits.

Instead of eliminating members of our customer service team, I needed to quickly hire more reps to keep up with the demand. I also warned my fulfillment center of the coming wave, and by some miracle, they managed to stay open without a major COVID-19 outbreak. I got a hold of Scott and asked how the production facility was looking over there. The news was good: they were already coming back down off of their first wave of the virus. I couldn't believe our luck. The factory was humming, the fulfillment center was hopping, and customers were coming to us in droves.

Our subscriber numbers exploded, and the revenues came pouring in. And it all happened *without increasing our advertising budget.* The upshot? Our acquisition cost for each customer dropped precipitously.

Pre-pandemic, we had been achieving an acquisition cost of around $50 per customer on a $10,000+ per day social media ad spend. But during the peak of COVID-19 lockdowns—from April, 2020 through August, 2020—three times as many customers were signing up. Our acquisition cost was cut to a third of what we were used to. It was like a fire sale on new subscribers. So we took advantage of the moment and upped our ad spending. We increased our spend to $15,000 a day. Then $20,000 a day. And we were getting *over a thousand* new subscribers every day.

Our revenues were bigger than ever, and because our customer acquisition costs were so low, more of our revenues were suddenly profits.

Throughout that spring and summer, I sometimes felt guilty when I spoke with other entrepreneurs. I was part of an organization for small business owners and startup leaders, and many of the other members had been forced to shut down or at least downsize their companies to operate with a skeleton crew. I'd listen to their tales of woe and think, "This is probably *not* a good time to mention my new boat."

By fall of 2020, I sat on that same sofa where I had experienced so many twists and turns, marveling at this stroke of good luck. It had been a dizzying 180-degree turn—from writing SinglesSwag's obituary to expanding our team and exceeding my wildest financial dreams.

I had finally done it. I had achieved what people had told me I couldn't. I had shot past all the naysayers and had built a thriving business. I relished the moment.

Maybe I'd finally get a new couch.

———

By August 2020, I was socking away $400,000 to $500,000 a month. Because I still owned 100 percent of the company, all of the profits went straight into my pocket. I sat on my couch letting my hair grow, letting my beard grow, and getting rich.

Jonathan and SinglesSwag featured in a full-page article in *Inc.* magazine (2020).

That's not to say that there weren't any challenges. There were definitely some speed bumps along the way. It turns out that it takes as much resilience to handle sudden success as it does to handle the hard times. When a sudden influx of new business comes your way, you still need to react with agility and creativity to ride the wave.

My biggest fear from the beginning of SinglesSwag was an inability to keep up with demand. There were some boxes that I researched that sold out every month and, while we used "selling out" as an attention-grabbing marketing pitch, SinglesSwag had never *truly* sold out. As a rule, we always ordered more product than we actually needed. If we projected that we'd need 30,000 boxes for a given month, we'd order enough product to fill 35,000 boxes, just to be safe. When COVID-19 hit, we suddenly needed to fill *50,000 boxes*. That's a huge change, and if we just stuck to the old ways of doing things, we could easily find ourselves out of inventory.

We had to do everything in our power to avoid telling people that we were simply "sold out" for May or June,. We wanted to send new members *something* while they were still excited and curious, rather than running the risk of them forgetting what they loved about SinglesSwag in the first place. So, we created a "Welcome Box" filled with some of our greatest hits of past products. Because these were all new subscribers, they hadn't seen these items before, and we knew these products would be well received because of strong customer feedback. We raided all of our product surplus from past months to put together the Welcome Boxes, which bought us some time to ramp up production.

I was on the phone with Scott night and day. I haggled, bargained, and begged them to get us more product.

We nearly doubled in size in just a couple of months, so of course there were snafus. For example, one of our shipping carriers was so overwhelmed by the spike in e-commerce orders during the lockdown that they lost a *full truckload* of our boxes. Over 5,000 of our boxes just disappeared. When I heard the news, I could have put my fist through a wall.

But I quickly let it go. I had to. With every bump in the road, I had to use all of my resilience to adapt and plow forward. I wanted to capitalize on this stroke of good fortune. There just wasn't time to dwell on any of the few opportunities I had missed—not when there was so much more opportunity to capitalize on out there.

When your business is booming, you'll need to be flexible and make quick decisions. You won't have time to get bogged down by the moments of adversity. Try a solution and move on. Then repeat again and again as you push forward.

This was one of the most stressful times in my life, but also one of the most exciting. Changes were coming at lightning speed, and we were adjusting on the fly. But the anxiety that came with our explosive growth was mitigated by the sweet sound of cash flooding into my bank account.

SinglesSwag was an enormous success, and so was I.

THE APPLE TAKES A BITE

They warned us it was coming.

It was going to be worse than the last recession, even worse than the financial meltdown of '08.

Apple iOS version 14.5.

This wasn't just a regular update for iPhones. This particular iOS update had one specific feature that they promised would change the landscape of digital advertising.

Users would now have a choice: they could *opt out* of apps tracking their activity. For users who were worried about privacy, it was a great development. No longer could apps take note of interests, browsing patterns, or purchase behavior. It made iPhone users feel more secure when they were online.

But it struck fear in the hearts of anyone advertising on Facebook.

Over the years, as I ramped up my Facebook ads from $10 to $20,000 a day, I was able to learn a lot about the ideal SinglesSwag customer. I had homed in on her age, her income, and what other subscription boxes she liked. I knew her hobbies, her tastes, and even her pet peeves.

With Facebook advertising, we were able to upload a sampling of that prized data for our 5,000 to 10,000 highest revenue subscribers. Facebook would create what they called a "Lookalike Audience"—up to ten million people who have similar demographics, buying behaviors, or interests as our ideal customer. With this information, we could target people who were interested in online shopping, *Vogue* magazine, or our competitors' boxes. It let SinglesSwag zero in on the exact people who would be most interested in our product, without wasting money and time on individuals who were not likely to purchase.

But with the new iOS, I would no longer have access to any of that critical data. I'd be flying blind.

Because we were spending millions per year on Facebook ads, we had a team of enterprise-level account managers at Facebook whose main job was to help us optimize advertising performance. Towards the end of 2020, they warned us that this new wrinkle had the potential to impact our marketing efforts.

But there wasn't much we could do. We were hurtling towards April 2021, the date when targeted ads for Apple users would become a thing of the past.

We didn't notice a huge difference when the new iOS first rolled out, and that makes sense: many users don't update their phones immediately. But as time went on, we started to see the effects. Finally, when Apple users were *forced* to update to the new iOS, there was a dramatic shift. Almost overnight, our ad campaigns became less and less effective.

The customer acquisition cost—which had dropped below $20 per customer—was now steadily climbing. It climbed past the bargain numbers of the lockdown and soared beyond even our pre-COVID-19 costs. The next thing we knew, it was costing us almost $300 to land just *one* new subscriber. Suddenly, advertising on Facebook—our primary source of customer acquisition—was no longer a viable strategy.

Our new subscriber numbers hit a plateau, so every time someone canceled, it felt like another drop of water seeping into a sinking ship. In the subscription box business, there is regular turnover of customers, often called "churn." Consumers typically either don't want to receive their boxes forever or can't afford to. Every subscription-based or recurring revenue business is forced to deal with churn. SinglesSwag had always gained many more customers than we lost each month, so churn was not an issue—until now. After the new iOS landed, we weren't able to acquire new customers as fast as we were losing existing customers. Our pre-pandemic standard was 200 to 300 new customers a day, but after the lockdowns ended and the new iOS rolled out, our numbers dropped to an anemic *forty* new customers a day.

It was a new world in digital advertising. And it was scary.

———

Even when SinglesSwag was experiencing a spike in new subscriptions, we knew that our rate of growth couldn't be sustained forever. We suspected that it would eventually level off and even decline a bit as the world reopened. But the expected post-lockdown downturn was compounded by the new Apple iOS.

The same resilience that helped me pilot SinglesSwag through our boom also helped me navigate the descent back to earth. The flexibility and creativity that helped us respond to a sudden increase in subscribers was also critical when we were forced to downsize and make challenging decisions that impacted our employees' and their families' lives. We had to quickly recognize that the "Lookalike" feature of Facebook advertising was no longer able to target our ideal consumer, and we had to adjust our spending to avoid pouring too much money into a losing strategy.

I don't want to give the impression that the end is nigh for the business I built. Far from it. Despite dipping from the eye-popping levels we reached during the pandemic, revenues at SinglesSwag are still strong. And the same proactive obsession that helped me scale the company the first time could be the key to re-scaling the company back to its peak. There are always new ideas and strategies to try.

I still have a few tricks up my sleeve.

But even if this business continues to decline, or the box subscription industry as a whole goes out of style with consumers, I've built far more than just a business. By growing and scaling my own company from nothing but an idea, I have built a skillset that can be applied to my next venture—and the one after that. And even more importantly, I've built confidence.

Often, it's a lack of confidence that keeps would-be entrepreneurs from pursuing their dreams. But through six years of incredible highs and lows, I've built a confidence that I could start with nothing again and create another highly successful venture. I know that I can carry this hard-won self-assurance with me into the next opportunity. I no longer live in fear. As I face whatever comes next, *nothing* will be holding me back.

I have the confidence that if something catastrophic happens to my business, I can repeat this level of success using the same process that I've already mastered. I now have a sense of calm because if the worst-case scenario does happen, I know I'll be able to do it all over again.

If you start a venture from nothing and scale it to a huge enterprise, you'll feel like a success. But if the advertising landscape changes or a recession hits, you may face a period of contraction. As painful as it may be, you may have to close locations, pivot to new ways of operating, or lay off employees in order to keep your business alive and thriving. If you are ever forced to downsize, you can't view it as a failure. Remember where you started and gauge your progress from where it all began. If you remember your humble beginnings, you'll realize that you are still a success—and no one can ever take that away from you.

WHEN THE STORM SUBSIDES

We've all seen those business posters with slogans designed to inspire entrepreneurs. *Courage, Persistence, Success*—with additional pithy quotes targeted at all of us dreamers. And while I've become immune to most of those messages, I must admit that there is one inspirational poster with a message that resonates with me deeply:

A smooth sea never made a skilled sailor.

That message hits close to home for me. In fact, I find it so profoundly meaningful that I've hung that poster in my bedroom where I can see it every morning and every night. That quote reminds me that every rocky patch I've endured in my life and career was preparing me for a later part of the journey. The turmoil I faced in my youth made me a better parent, friend, and entrepreneur. The rough seas I faced when I launched my business toughened me up to handle the challenges of growth. In turn, those challenges readied me for the rough seas of an eventual downturn and whatever will come next.

When you're building a business, not everything will go smoothly, but those rough seas will prepare you for what's next. Those difficult times will teach you new skills and give you a broad knowledge that can be applied to all kinds of future challenges. Your healthy obsession forced you to look at problems from every angle, and that ability will help you make more out of the rest of your life, even if your current venture doesn't succeed.

Business is changing every day. What works brilliantly one month might fall flat the next. And remember, exponential growth doesn't last forever. At some point growth tends to level off, and you'll need to explore new products, new features, or entirely new ideas in order to maintain momentum. Some ideas have their moment in time and then fade in popularity as the novelty wears off for consumers. But even if your business has a finite life cycle, it doesn't mean that you are finished as an entrepreneur. If you have built something from nothing, you'll have the confidence it takes to launch another business—and another, and another.

And if you haven't achieved success yet, that's okay, too. *Trying counts.* Every idea you pursue will lead you to new opportunities to learn and grow. Even if you have attempted to launch a business multiple times and haven't succeeded yet, you haven't failed, either. You've *learned.* The important thing is to employ that hard-won knowledge in future ventures.

After six years of growing SinglesSwag into a successful enterprise, I feel like I have a Ph.D. in marketing, management, communications, customer research, and a dozen other areas. I'm ready for whatever comes next. Whether it's re-scaling SinglesSwag, opening a consulting firm, or taking on a new business that I haven't even dreamed up yet, I'm ready to tackle any challenge. My first entrepreneurial success wasn't the end of my story.

It was only the beginning.

After navigating the roughest of all seas, my skills are honed. It's time to lay out a map, plot a course, and set sail for new lands.

It's time for the next adventure to begin.

KEY TAKEAWAYS

- **Learn** that in your entrepreneurial or professional journey, there will be difficult circumstances that you cannot predict or control. It's okay to obsess at these times, it's okay to catastrophize, it's okay to be scared. Everything in your business and in your life will happen for a reason. The rough seas and smooth waters along your journey will make you a stronger entrepreneur and person.

- **Reflect** on the potential events and issues that could impact your business or brand. Are there any preemptive measures you can take to mitigate these concerns to protect yourself, your employees, and your business? Go down the rabbit hole and see where it takes you. Could you be surprised like I was during the COVID-19 lockdown and go from fear of losing it all to game-changing wealth overnight?

- **Act.** That's it. Just act. If you have already acted and haven't achieved success yet, that's okay. Trying matters. Every idea you pursue will lead to new opportunities to learn and grow. Failing is okay, as long as you learn from it. I'm confident you have a business or product idea and likely multiple ideas. There will never be a better time than now to *act*.

CONCLUSION

My natural tendency in life is to look forward. Before I became an entrepreneur, I was always dreaming of better days. When I did finally launch my own business, I was so consumed by making it a success that I never had the time or bandwidth to take stock of what I had been through.

But in writing this book, I've been forced to look back on my journey—to explore the roller coaster I've been on and the obstacles I've overcome. It has helped me understand myself, and how all the things that have happened to me make up who I am. All of the pieces of me—the strengths, the broken bits, and the parts that are still evolving—influenced decisions many years later. When you're an entrepreneur, you can't factor yourself out of your business. In many ways, you *are* your business. Taking stock has helped me recognize the mistakes I've made but has also pointed out what I've done right.

There are stories in this book that I've never told anyone. I'm opening up so that you can see a more realistic portrait of a successful entrepreneur—including the parts that aren't very pretty. Whenever I've been interviewed by the press or for other media, I've always projected the positivity and confidence that seemed fitting for my flourishing company. But that image was never the whole story. With this book, I hope to give a clearer picture of who I am and the complex backstory to my success.

Because hiding the struggle really does a disservice to anyone who hopes—but doubts—that they can also be successful. I didn't have many good role models for entrepreneurship, and it always felt like the people who succeeded had so many advantages already. I hope that by sharing my story, you can take heart in the truth: you can succeed in your dream without a conventional business background or any help other than your own fierce determination to make it work.

I admit that part of the motivation for writing this book was to show all the haters and doubters that they were flat-out wrong about me. I wanted all the people who had treated me like a piece of shit throughout my life to read this book and have my success rubbed in their faces.

But now that I see my story in black-and-white, I realize it is so much more than a revenge tale.

I want this book to help aspiring entrepreneurs and anyone who wants to break out of an unsatisfying life. I hope that it finds its way onto the shelf of someone who's fighting depression or some dreamer who has to listen to naysayers and doubters every day.

And when you close this book, I want you to remember several big lessons:

- **Don't just follow the expected path, asleep at the wheel.** It's never too late to realize that this is *your* life and that you can steer it in any direction you'd like.

- **Find a healthy obsession.** Take the energy you put into negative obsessions (a frustrating job or stressful finances) and focus on a new idea that could pay off emotionally and financially.

- **Don't wait for the perfect idea.** An original idea isn't necessary. As long as you're passionate about your healthy obsession, you can make it a success.

- **Face your fear of rejection and ridicule.** Be vulnerable enough to announce your idea to the world. It's the only way to get on the path to success.

- **Ignore the haters, and you will eventually find your admirers.** If your idea doesn't connect with people right away, that's okay. Not everyone will get it, and that's also okay. If you hold onto your belief, the idea will eventually find the right audience.

- **Don't listen to the naysayers.** There will be no shortage of people telling you it can't be done, why it will never work, or giving you unsubstantiated advice. Be confident that you can do this—*without* deep-pocketed investors, fancy degrees, or lots of employees.

- **If you're willing to learn new skills, you can wear every hat.** Your business will eventually grow too large to do it all by yourself, but in the early days, learning to execute every role well will better equip you to be a more effective leader.

- **When you can no longer do it alone, delegate to someone you trust.** Have the courage to hand off some of the responsibilities that are holding you back from focusing on strategy and growth.

- **Learn from your mistakes.** It's inevitable that you'll occasionally make bad decisions, but those missteps will teach you a lot. Use those lessons to weather the next storm.

- **You don't need a Harvard MBA or a rich family; you just need a desire to change your life.** If you're willing to throw your whole self—your passion, drive, and obsession—into your project, you *will* improve your life.

I've shared my story, bared my soul, and revealed my most embarrassing mistakes so that you, the reader, would understand this simple truth: you can do the same thing I did.

Jonathan at his home, Boca Raton, Florida (2021).

If I could become a multimillionaire despite the limitations I faced, *so can you*. If I could start with only $2,000 and generate $60 million in revenue in six years, *so can you*. If I could reach 350,000 customers starting from a sole proprietorship with no employees, *so can you*. If I could go against conventional wisdom and the so-called "rules" of business and succeed *my* way, *so can you*.

Regardless of what your objective is—starting a business, overcoming depression, losing weight, or running a triathlon—the lesson is still the same. This book should serve as proof that obstacles can be overcome. I was a divorced dad with a history of mental illness and no passion for my career. Yet I was able to unleash the power of healthy obsessions to change my life.

And so can you.

DECISION TIME

When you set out to change your life, there will be hundreds, maybe even thousands, of difficult moments. You will face challenges every day that will make you want to give up. And giving up is always an option.

Giving up is easy.

Every single day, you will have the option to just sit on the sofa and watch TV instead of taking proactive steps towards launching your venture. You can choose the easier path of going to a bar and hanging out with friends instead of staying at home and learning a new skill.

You can decide to do *nothing*, or you can decide to do *something*.

You are free to do as you please. But I want you to know: if you decide to take the easier path, you are accepting a life of mediocrity. On the other hand, if you choose the harder path—the healthy obsession, the long hours of work, and the late nights learning—it will improve your world. It won't be easy, but by making these sacrifices, you can experience a rewarding, meaningful, and life-changing adventure.

When you put down this book, it will be time to choose.

I hope you choose action. I hope you take even one little step towards something bold and new. Even if that one action is just brainstorming ideas, it's still an action.

Your first action could even be to reach out to me at *Jonathan Beskin.com*. You can let me know which parts of my story resonated with you or share with me something similar that you've experienced.

I grew up as one of the have-nots in a town full of rich kids. As an adult, I was the guy who couldn't figure out what to do with his career, the guy who rolled through life on autopilot. I was the guy who wasn't good at taking advice, the guy who thought he could start a successful enterprise with just $2,000.

I guess you could say I'm about the least likely millionaire there is.

Then again, maybe it's not me at all.

Maybe the least likely millionaire is *you*.

ACKNOWLEDGMENTS

To my mother, Mary Beskin, my biggest cheerleader and most valuable confidant. You are brilliant, having graduated high school early at sixteen and completed both undergraduate and graduate degrees by age twenty-one. You could have been successful at any career or endeavor, but chose a selfless path as an elementary school teacher for forty years, impacting the lives of countless students and improving the skillset of numerous junior colleagues through your guidance and mentorship. You did not hesitate when I asked you to retire early in the middle of a school year because I was in desperate need of help with my rapidly growing venture. You have proven yourself to be a dynamic executive leader and an invaluable asset. You have been there for me through every up and down of my life, and I am incredibly grateful for the many sacrifices you have made for me. I love you.

To my son and best friend, everything I do in business and life is for you. You are bright, caring, kind, and diversely talented.

You have already achieved so much in life, and I am beyond excited to see what your future holds and what you will accomplish. I love you more than anything.

To Charlie Schneider, whose life was cut tragically short. You lived an inspired life and left behind a meaningful legacy for your family, friends, and employees. I always valued your advice and enjoyed the time we spent together.

To Maggie, my Victorian Bulldog. You are my most consistent companion and love unconditionally. I hope you know how truly loved and cared for you are.

ABOUT THE AUTHOR

Serial entrepreneur Jonathan Beskin built his first company, a women's lifestyle subscription box, from a pre-revenue idea to over $60 million in revenue in six years. An investor in multiple private companies and startups, he has twice been featured in the prestigious *Inc.* 5000 list. Beskin is a digital advertising and e-commerce expert; he often speaks at conferences and academic institutions. He holds an MBA in finance from Florida Atlantic University.

Printed in the USA
CPSIA information can be obtained
at www.ICGtesting.com
LVHW040306120923
757935LV00016B/513/J